TWO [...] MY FRI[...]

A cracked glass of pub humour compiled by **Brian Glover** and **Neil Hanson**

Printed and bound in Great Britain by Hazell Watson & Viney Limited,
Member of the BPCC Group, Aylesbury, Bucks

THANKS

Thanks to the major contributors—Alan Coren, Nigel Forde, Miles Kington, Bill Lythgoe, Roger Protz and Keith Waterhouse—for their written articles. And special thanks to *Punch* magazine.

Thanks to Hector Breeze, Honeysett, Terry Hughes, Dai Owen, Ken Pyne, Reading, John Simpson, Bill Tidy, George Woods and the other cartoonists.

Thanks to the writers of the It Makes You Think column in *What's Brewing* over the years—P. A. Newton, S. O'Brierty and Miles Brewster. Their fan will be interested to learn that P. A. Newton is still conducting a one-man swim-in at a Highland distillery. He will come out of the whisky vat when the Stuarts are restored to the throne. S. O'Brierty has returned to his previous job as a taster for Guinness in Dublin, while the current columnist, Miles Brewster, is mailing his scrumpy-spattered copy from the Dr. Duckfoot Clinic for the Permanently Inebriated in Plymouth.

Thanks also to the Beat the Cistern column in *Mersey Drinker* and our many intrepid pub loo investigators for the graffiti.

Right, lads. What are we going to do wi' rest o' Arts Council grant?

THE PUB is the great repository of completely useless information; if you want to know Don Bradman's inside leg measurement or the average diameter of a Great Auk's egg, ask around your local. Even more valuable is its role as the Exchange&Mart of jokes. About 90% of the British gross national merriment is invented in pubs and bartered in exchange for a pint.

Keep your ear to the ground and you'll hear the best and worst tales in the world. You're also likely to get a cigarette end up your nostril, but that's a small price to pay. For those who haven't time to hang around taprooms, we've produced this slim volume to stir a few happy memories.

Brian Glover, Neil Hanson

● Brian Glover is the Editor of Publications for CAMRA, responsible for the Campaign's monthly newspaper What's Brewing. Neil Hanson is the editor of CAMRA's Good Beer Guide and author of Classic Country Pubs. Both have been known, on rare occasions, to prop up bars, telling strange tales. Fortunately, they were unable to remember any of them for inclusion in this book.

MAN UTD
MORRIS
MEN

Tiny problem

SHIRLEY Pepper, the saintly madonna who runs the world's smallest pub, the Nutshell in Bury St. Edmunds, is having a spot of bother with the council.

It appears that Suffolk environmental health regulations dictate that she must have a refuse bin on the premises. As anyone who has visited the 14′ × 8′ premises will tell you, it is hard enough squeezing in the drip trays.

But St. Edmondsbury Council Officials think they have found a solution. The new official dustbin sits proudly on the top shelf, twelfth curio from the right.

Made from regulation green plastic and of the precise approved design, it measures three inches high and one-inch in diameter.

Little nip

IT brought a whole new meaning to the phrase "I'll just have a little nip", when a drinker in Brighton poured himself a bottle of Merrydown vintage cider—and found three dead earwigs in his glass.

Coughing up

SO now we know why the big brewers, with their overriding concern for the general good, introduced weak, pricy lager: it was the help combat drunken driving.

Thanks to lager, Brian Yeo of Hampshire escaped a driving ban, even though he was over the top when breathalysed by the local constabulary.

Brian drank five pints of lager then called at his girlfriend's, where he had three swigs from a bottle of cough mixture. He was later apprehended by the police and charged following some deep breathing exercises with a small plastic bag.

When he appeared at Southampton Crown Court, he admitted that he did not know that a bottle of cough mixture contained the equivalent of one and a half whiskies.

Quoth the Recorder, Barry Carter: "I am satisfied it was the cough mixture that took you over the top."

Keep taking the Venos.

Mild delight

THE wonders of ale . . . Bob and Janet Gascoyne of Cheadle Heath Cheshire had been trying to start a family for four years.

Then the landlord of their local, the Printer's Arms, suggested that Bob switched from bitter to mild. Lorry driver Bob took his advice, had a few pints of the dark delicious, and went home for an early night.

Lo and behold, wife Janet announced a few weeks later that a small Gascoyne was on the way. "Mild . . . the beer that stimulates parts that other beers cannot reach?"

No score

ARTHUR Booth, 78, has drunk 20 pints a day, every day, for the past 60 years, and all at The Clarence in Hastings.

"A doctor once told me that every time you have sex you lose a pint of blood and every time you have a drink you gain a pint—so I stuck to beer. I've never had sex and I've never wanted to. Staying single has saved me a fortune. It's how I afford my beer. I've got all my own teeth," said Arthur.

Schmuck's fizz

IF you want bubbly without the bite, Matthews International Trading of Pennsylvania have brought us "Champayne"—the completely new sparkling drink that "looks and tastes like real champagne", but contains no alcohol.

Honestly, weddings are bad enough without having to savour the prospect of being sober for the best man's speech.

Taxing time

THE TRIALS and tribulations of running a pub: David and Pat Brandon are licensees of the 17th-century Dolphin Inn at Newport Pagnell, Buckinghamshire.

A Customs and Excise officer arrived at the Dolphin soon after the Brandon children had finished their breakfast at a bar table, used for convenience as it is next to the kitchen.

"Who's been eating on licensed premises?" demanded the VAT man. Pat Brandon explained it was her children, but the excise inspector was unmoved.

"You should charge your children for any meals they consume on licensed premises," he pontificated—and added that they should pay VAT on top.

Then David Brandon's father came downstairs and was told he should be paying for the cup of coffee he was drinking—plus VAT, of course.

Unmoved by the Brandon's protestations the inspector continued his examination of the pub's lunch of lobster soup, trout and coffee. The lunch was on the house but the gracious VAT man pointed out: "You should really have charged me for that—it involves VAT."

In the event, he decided not to pursue his demand for VAT payments for the Brandon's meals and the official Customs and Excise line is that he interpreted the law too rigidly.

But landlords beware. If an even more officious VAT man visits your pub, hide the cornflakes.

Bomb the ban

MRS Bean, who runs the Three Horseshoes in Upper Heyford, Oxfordshire, has a sign outside her pub saying "Polite Notice. No CND supporters welcome".

Explaining her ban on 38 per cent of the country's population, Mrs B. said: "Everyone's entitled to their views—that's why my parents went to war."

Last gasp

MIND HOW you go in the West Country. In a feature on beer, the Bath and West Evening Chronicle says of keg beer: "It keeps for much longer, is filtered and is often chilled and pasteurised.

"It is pushed through the pumps with carbon *monoxide* dispensed from cylinders, so it's fizzy."

And probably deadly.

The eyes have it

IF you've ever cycled or staggered with the aid of a torch from the pub to your home late at night, you have had reason to bless Percy Shaw, the man who invented cat's eyes, the road studs that reflect light.

Shaw died in 1976 at the age of 86 with a million or two in the bank. Legend had it that Percy, something of a tippler in his time, got the idea for his invention when his car lights picked out the tramlines in the middle of the road as he returned home in his native Halifax.

When the tramlines were ripped up in the 1930s he decided to manufacture reflecting road studs. They made him a rich man, but he remained true to the simple things in life.

He lived in a house without carpets or curtains. But he had three Rolls-Royce motor cars—and a cellar full of crates of Worthington White Shield.

Percy, in the great cat's eye in the sky, might disagree, but it is claimed that you can get sufficiently lit up on a few bottles of White Shield to find your way home without the benefit of road studs.

Refreshes the . . .

I AM thinking of producing a catalogue of useful things to do with lager.

The latest idea comes from Karen Harrison, an administrative person at Whitbread Wessex. She has found that Heineken is particularly good at fixing leaking car radiators.

When her frosted Ford blew a leak recently she topped up with a four-pack of the canned hair restorer and managed to drive ten miles to the nearest garage.

House comic

IT'S good to see that the nice line in wit in the House of Commons did not die with Disraeli. Blyth Valley MP, John Ryman, in a debate on our laughable licensing laws, quipped:

"Statistics have been used in this debate rather as a drunk uses a lamp post —for support rather than illumination."

Playing dodgems

IN these days of soaring beer prices, the practice of getting out of buying your round is becoming even more sophisticated, with drinkers in the southern stockbroker belts claiming that their inability to replenish the glasses stems from the fact that they left their cheque cards at home.

Our favourite tale concerns the young man who just refused point blank to stand his corner. Night after night, he would hurry up to the pub with his pals, cheerfully sup up their proffered pints and then gaze fixedly at the ceiling when his turn came round.

His "friends" quickly tired of this uncharitable behaviour. One night, noticing a pound note sticking out of his rear pocket, a member of the group light-fingered the greenback, went to the bar and bought a round (and the fact that he could buy a round with just one pound indicates a certain age to this tale).

Misery Guts swigged his new pint, grunted "cheers" and inquired who had bought the round.

"You did!" the assembled worthies shouted, all pointing the finger of derision at him.

Whereupon the young man burst into tears and ran sobbing from the pub.

Jack the lad

Here's to the man who calls everyone "Jack",
Here's to a jolly good fellow,
Here's to the chap who likes knocking it back
And doesn't knock off till he's mellow.
Once they are downed,
He'll borrow a pound
And make for the loo when it's his round!

ANOTHER tight tale is even older and comes from the East Midlands:

They called him "Baggy", on account of when he was a lad he played a mean game of soccer in voluminous shorts. Hell of a nice bloke—a real gent—but somehow missed out fairly frequently when it was his round.

He'd been fishing with three mates and, traditionally, they called in at a workingman's club on Sunday lunchtime for a few jars and a game of solo after the morning out.

Jack bought a round.

"It's your round."

Fred bought a round. Sam bought a round. Baggy went out the back to turn his bike round.

So Jack popped for another. Fred followed. Sam weighed in with a second. Baggy went to ring his missus.

There was a rumble from the lads, involving the steward in a discussion about the "tight old so-and-so".

Anyway, Baggy came back and dealt the cards. Jack called abundance. Fred called open misere. Sam beamed. "I'll go the lot," he said, laying down 13 spades.

"Stuff me," said Baggy, "and here's me sat with 13 diamonds!"

Fred winked at the steward. "What d'you say, Baggy?—Thirteen diamonds?"

Baggy agreed emphatically—and almost before he could lay his cards on the table, the steward confronted him with a tray holding 13 uncapped bottles of Double Diamond and a demand for 19s. 6d. . . .

It was, of course, a few years ago. But true.

Only here for . . .

THERE would be no civilisation without beer. That's the sobering thought from American anthropologist Dr. Solomon Katz, who believes when neolithic man accidentally discovered the brewing process, he swapped his nomadic, animal hunting life to become a crop grower.

Private bar

ACCORDING to the Enfield Advertiser, a Watney pub in Edmonton, North London, the Cart Overthrown, has been revamped with the following improvements: "The ladies toilets have been very tastefully decorated, there are plants and a small raised stage where live country and western music can be heard from Thursday to Sunday."

Wordsmith

A WHAT'S Brewing scout passing the Hanley Arms in Hornsey Lane, North London, slammed on the brakes when he saw a new legend over the door: "John Smith". He had never supped the Northern brew and hurried inside.

He was a trifle miffed to be confronted by the usual grisly array of Watney pressure taps. Undaunted, he told the barperson: "A pint of John Smith's, please."

"Do what?" was the reply. He repeated the question.

"John Smith, mate," he was told, "is the name of the landlord."

"You'll have to throw him back in—it's his round!"

KEITH WATERHOUSE

Shoot the landlord

IF I WERE guest dictator of Britain for a day and allowed to have 100 people lined up against a wall and shot, I think upon mature reflection I'd choose the landlords, managers and proprietors of my unfavourite pubs.

In taking this extreme but necessary step I would not be condemning them for the inefficiency, discomfort or sheer bloody awfulness of the premises they preside over. Nor for their complicity in advertising fresh hot snacks when all they have to offer is warmed-up pies. Nor for their guilt in letting glasses pile up on the tables to the point at which their customers get the illusion of drinking in a sump-pit. I'd overlook their churlishness to strangers and their grovelling sycophancy to regulars.

What would qualify them for the firing squad—and they wouldn't have the option of a fine—would be their lamentable, abominable, unbelievably hideous taste. Bad taste—the total absence of any sense of colour, composition, proportion, or light and shade, or indeed any conception at all of what gives life its quality of being worth the living. Something that has for long been a blight on our national landscape.

You see it in every High Street furniture store and on every council housing development, in every amusement arcade, on bleak factory estates and in the crowded souvenir shops of Blackpool and Southend. But nowhere do you find it in a more concentrated form than in the English public house.

If there is a pub in Britain whose landlord has even a primitively-developed sense of decoration, I have yet to find it. If there is any other vocation believing that a tartan carpet will sit happily with Regency-striped wallpaper bedecked with pictures of vintage cars, I have yet to come across it. The average pub is so monumentally awful in its decor that you could shift it, brick by brick and

beer-mat by beer-mat, into the Victoria and Albert Museum as a permanent exhibition of all that is ghastly in British design.

It can't be accidental. It's got to be deliberate. It's as if the landlords of Britain had held a convention and voted for the most grisly wallpaper, the most garish lighting, the type of plastic table most likely to tilt like a rocking-horse when you lean on it, the kind of carpeting—all dots, bars and oblongs—most likely to make the customer feel he is in the first stages of delirium tremens. There must have been a show of hands to decide what particular electric advertising display would best induce spots before the eyes; and whether bright yellow tiles or stippled lime-green would be the most vomit-inducing effect for the gent's lavatory. And what particular design of corrugated-hardboard pelmet over the bar would most make the regulars wish their pub had been blown up by Irish terrorists.

"Has anyone any thoughts about ice-buckets?" I can hear the chairman saying. An immediate, eager suggestion from the delegate from the Fox and Hounds: "How about in the shape of a pineapple?" Carried unanimously.

"And what about those little price-tags we stick in the cheese sandwiches? Any suggestions for improving those?"

"They could be in the form of galleons, or cockerels," suggests the delegate from the Goat in Boots, dreamily. "Made out of plastic. In subdued, tasteful colours, such as purple, violet, orange, raspberry or perhaps mauve." Carried unanimously.

"Table-lamps?" Up jumps the representative of the Pig and Whistle, Adam's apple bobbing over his Royal Engineers cravat in the nervousness of the moment. "Supposing—it's only a suggestion—that we make them out of Chianti bottles?"

Carried unanimously, with prolonged cheers. And so (I must imagine) this deathly conference went on, dedicated to spreading bad taste throughout the land. By popular acclaim, dartboards, dominoes and bar-billiard tables were thrown out on the promise of piped music and fruit-machines. Marble-topped tables, good for another century's wear and tear and no less easy to clean than plastic, were disposed of to the junk-shops.

Draught bitter from the barrel was abolished, on condition that a miniature representation of the non-existent barrel would henceforth be incorporated on the beer-pump. Those landlords who owned genuine Tudor beams agreed to disguise them with plasterboard in case they should be accused of being old-fashioned; those who had only plasterboard ceilings were urged to install fake Tudor beams lest their pubs should lack atmosphere.

If you think I'm being unkind, have a look at what they've done to your own local or, if they haven't done it yet, go to someone else's local and see what they're doing to that. Look at some of the renovated pub façades that look more like laundrettes than licensed premises.

Behind it all, on the part of the people who rip the guts out of perfectly good pubs to make them look like bus station waiting rooms, is the fear of "getting out of touch". The public (so this reasoning goes) want supermarkets instead of corner shops, and Wimpey bars instead of corner cafes. They want bingo halls and discotheques and boutiques.

Consequently, in these sophisticated, hurrying years, when they go for a drink in the evenings they must want something different from what they've been getting already. Wheel in the tartan carpet, the pineapple ice-bucket (though never mind the ice) and the pictures of vintage cars. Wheel out the dartboard and the piano; and the old regulars, too, if they insist on singing.

No doubt market research proves that there is some new breed of drinker—the offspring, very probably, of all

those hearty young men in blazers who used to swig pink gins in suburban roadhouses in the 1930s. This breed demands fluorescent lights and paper towels in the loo, or at least a rack where paper towels might be if the management could be bothered to replace them. It wants beer-mats in the shape of maple-leaves, amusing ash-trays, leatherette settees, warmed-up pies, and music which nobody notices until it's switched off like the keg lager at closing time.

A couple of years ago I was in the perfect English pub. It had real oak beams, beer from the wood, a place for darts and another for shove ha'penny, good food, a landlord who welcomed his customers and a barman who made sure that they sat down at a clean table. I can't go back to this place very often, since it was in Los Angeles.

Keith Waterhouse

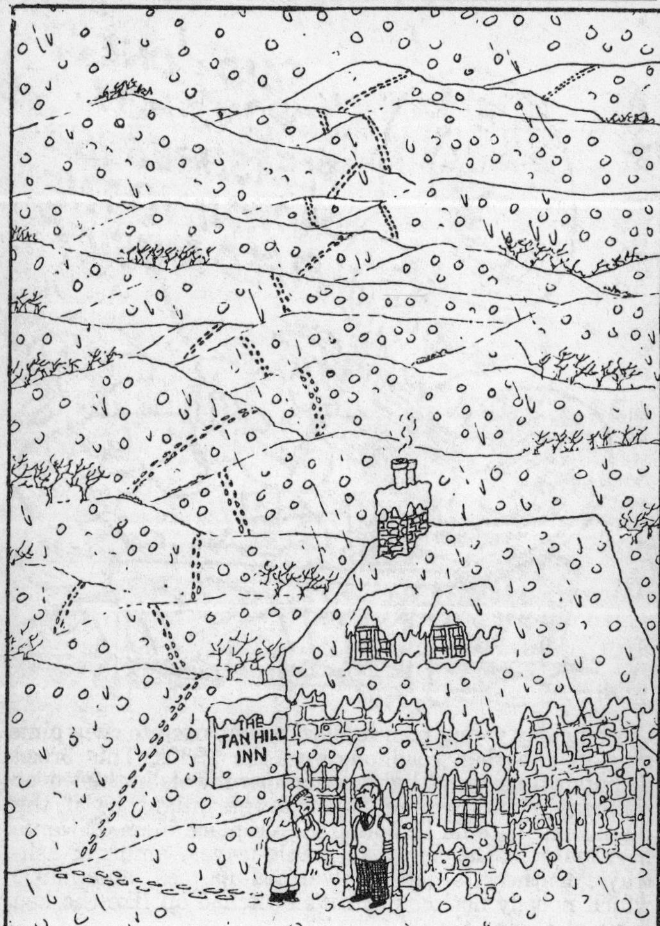

"I'm afraid last orders were five minutes ago– you'll have to come back at seven o'clock"

Secret drinkers

WILLIAM Rathje, a Professor from the University of Arizona, has applied himself to the vital task of examining the contents of the whole town's garbage cans.

In the town, where 85% of those surveyed said that they did not drink beer, 75% were found to have empty beer cans in their household refuse. He concludes that people lie about what they drink.

Sober thought

I HAVE been reading a history of the Empire and am moved to tell you the salutory tale of Sir Horace Frampton.

I could do with a swim.

He and his wife Lady Bertha were sent to the South Seas Colonies at the end of the last century to educate the natives. She was of the tee-total persuasion, and after much haranguing forced her husband to stick to Adam's Ale.

Alas, poor man, a few months after taking this pledge he died from cholera. He had caught it from drinking water.

Recommended

THE beermats in The Plough, Tyttenhanger Green, near St. Albans, read: *"We specialise in incompetent staff, greasy food and exorbitant prices in a terrible atmosphere. Purveyors of murky beers and watery spirits in short measures. Not recommended by Egon Ronay, the English Tourist Board or CAMRA."*

The joke has now backfired on licensee Mike Barrowman. The Plough has been named Pub-of-the-Month by the S. Herts. branch of CAMRA.

Clever brew

A NAME to add to our list of silly titles for ersatz lager; the Guernsey Brewery produces a brew called Hi Brau.

Person ale

THE following was seen in a pub recently, scrawled on the wall: MANN's (Sex Discrimination Act)—Persons; BROWN (Race discrimination Act)—Ethnic; ALE (Trades Description Act)—Carbonated Liquid. Now there's a drink. Bottle of Person's Ethnic Liquid.

No Red

AS the dust has long settled on the Warrington by-election, we can pass on a campaign story that cannot open us to accusations of political bias.

Entering a Greenall Whitley tavern, the SDP candidate, "Woy's the Boy" Jenkins, was asked what he would like. Conscious of the fact that Warrington is a proletarian and brewing stronghold, Mr Jenkins asked for a pint of beer. Such a request being as vague as the SDP manifesto, he was asked to specify the type.

"Oh, dwy white, please."

Mother's Plide

INTERESTING to note that in China beer is officially classified as "liquid bread". It's worth remembering next time you're stopped and asked to blow into the dreaded balloon: "Sorry, ossifer, I've had one slice over the eight."

Stout meal

MOONEY'S Bar are offering a seven course, traditional Irish dinner—a boiled potato and six pints of Guinness . . .

Spiked!

"NEWS has just arrived of the county's latest small brewing venture. The Hedgehog Brewery, started by A. F. Day and his wife April, has been set up in an old shoe shop in Watford. The shop used to be a pub so the cellar has proved invaluable. 'Neither of us are brewers, but April used to be a tea-lady before we were married,' quipped Alf.

"At first they will brew just one beer, Clarke's Special, which will have an original gravity somewhere between 1030 and 1055. 'Current production is six pints,' says April, 'but we hope to raise that to seven or eight by the end of the week.' Distribution is being kept down to pubs within a 150-mile radius and their dray, a converted 1970 Ford Transit sporting the brewery's logo of a hedgehog rampant over a tea-urn, can often be seen being towed into pub car-parks and various garages in the county.

"Quality, as usual, is a major problem for the small brewer, since Alf is only 4 feet 6 inches tall and can't see over the sides of the mash tun. 'We realise that there may be a few duff batches in the first few months, but we should be able to increase this number considerably by the end of the year,' says Alf. 'We have a considerable price advantage over our larger competitors, however. With the beer costing only 6 or 7 pence a pint to brew you should be able to pick up a pint of Clarke's for under £1·80.

"CAMRA's liaison officer with the brewery, who drank the whole first week's production himself, says the beer has a 'light, hoppy bite'. We look forward to trying the beer when April can get down to Boots for some more malt extract."

● This item was culled from the April (repeat April) edition of the CAMRA Hertfordshire Newsletter—and repeated in the licensed fools paper, The Morning Advertiser!

"No tray, thanks – I've enough to carry as it is"

Fuels rush in

WATCH out for some surprise brewery takeover bids from Shell and Esso.

The idea is not as daft as it sounds, since recent announcements indicate that the petroleum and beer industries are moving closer together.

One Euro MP has suggested that the EEC's huge wine lake could be drained away by mixing the rough wine with petrol, once it has been distilled into ethyl alcohol, for use in cars.

While Radio Budapest has reported (no kidding) that a Hungarian oil refinery is to be converted into a brewery by the end of the year.

Pint of multi-grade please, barman, and two shots of Redex.

Horse play

AT the opening of the Chiswell Street Vaults in London, Nicholas Windrum of Whitbread says "the famous Whitbread Shire horses will be pulling a period dray just as they did in 1742 when Sam Whitbread commenced brewing".

Is this a case for the RSPCA—making 237-year-old horses pull heavy loads around?

Surprise delivery

HOPEFULLY, Mr. Peter Beck and his family have recovered from the unconvential beer delivery he received from Websters Brewery of Halifax to his pub, the Punchbowl in Elland, West Yorkshire.

A Webster's tanker carrying beer to Wilsons Brewery in Manchester careered out of control into the side of the pub and deposited nearly 1,500 gallons into Mr. Beck's cellar. A further 2,500 gallons gushed out onto the streets of Elland.

"Lucky, wasn't it?"

The P factor

ACCORDING to an unimpeachable source, a research team at Newcastle hospital is undertaking a special investigation of a problem known as "urodynamics" or piddling to the great unwashed masses.

The team has established, without fear of contradiction, that excessive beer drinking can lead to incontinence. We would have thought that, in the interests of saving public money, the Government could have established this fact by visiting the Members' Bar of the House of Commons any night—but we digress.

This most fascinating outcome of this bladder-boggling investigation is the news that excessive carbon dioxide in keg beer causes greater wetting of the inside trouser leg than cask-conditioned beer.

The Tyneside branch of CAMRA (who have reason to be more concerned than most) are now demanding that the Government issue a health warning to the effect that keg beers can seriously damage your Y-fronts.

Two pee on beer

AFTER arranging a brewery trip round Sam Smiths of Tadcaster, landlord Tony Bevington of Middlesbrough's Cambridge Hotel was ashamed to find that two members of the party, having quaffed a few too many free samples, proceeded to relieve themselves into a 1,200 gallon tank of bitter.

Sams were not amused as they flushed away £7,000 worth of ale.

Late drinker

HAVE you ever worried about the state of pub toilets? Well you can worry a good deal more after you have heard the unfortunate tale of Les Pallett.

A regular at the Good Beer Guide listed Bricklayers Arms in Icknield Port Road, Birmingham, Mr Pallett was indulging in a pre-Christmas celebration. A visit to the gentleman's cloakroom was, however, interrupted by his sudden death.

Everyone has to die somewhere, you may be thinking, and what better place than your local? What turns the tragedy into a black comedy, however, is that his body was not found for seven days.

In future all GBG inspectors are asked to look under the doors of the cubicles.

Scots flush

A special "Guid Bog Guide to Edinburgh pubs", described the conveniences in the Covenanters as: "Wee and clean."

Windy stop

GREAT misprints of our time: the London Country bus timetable for the Dorking area kindly includes bus stops outside local hostelries such as the White Horse. Users of the 425 route will be interested to learn that they can hail an omnibus outside the Star and Farter.

Cock-up

HEINEKON, Whitbread's pseudo-Dutch lager, was blushing all over its clever commercials after an improper suggestion.

The beer which is reputed to refresh the parts other beers never consider, has been sponsoring a clean-up of the Cerne Giant, a huge fertility figure carved in the chalk hillside near Dorchester. And it had been suggested that Whitbread might use the Giant in one of their "before and after" adverts.

But they dropped the idea when someone pointed out that, once the grass was cleared away, a certain part of the figure's anatomy was a little too explicit.

A.C.A.B.
KILLJOY WAS HERE
DS!
SP
I THINK ∴ I AM
I'm pink ∴ I'm spam
I OINK ∴ I'M HAM
I RUN ∴ im CRAM
FRENCH DOCKERS RULE - AUX QUAIS
Today's tongue twister! Cunnilingus
SPANIARDS RULE OLE!
KS
Dyslexics rule - KO
CAFÉ RULES - AU LAIT
Scotland rules - och aye
Shylock rules - Oy Vey!
HUMPTY DUMPTY WAS PUSHED!

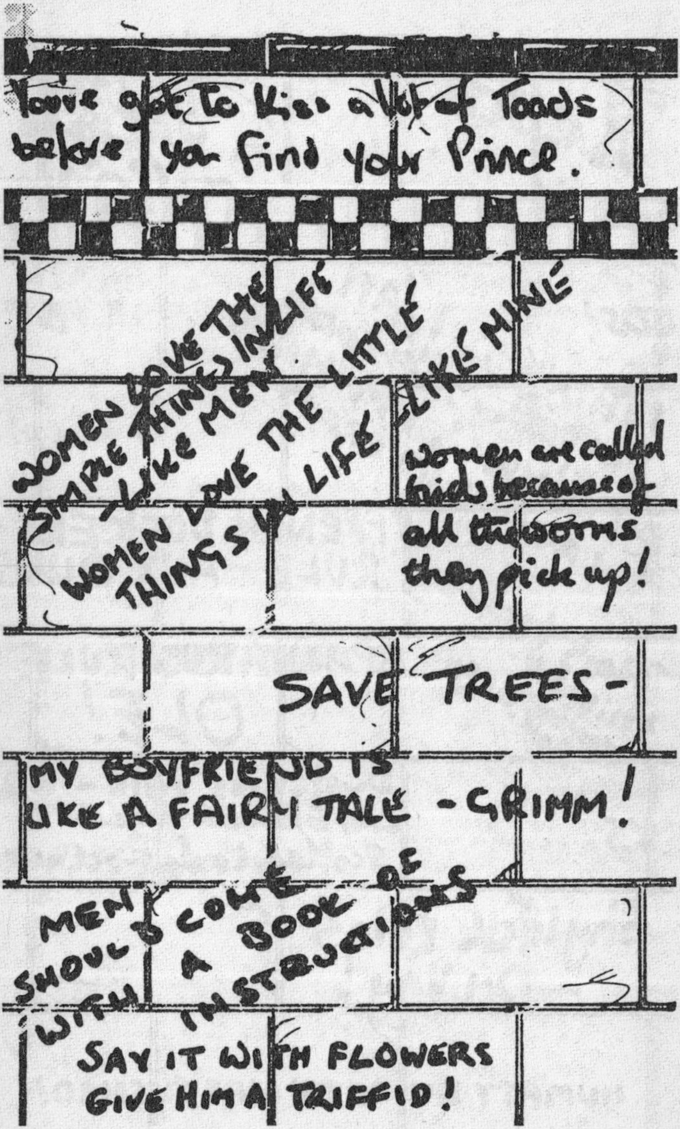
You've got to Kiss a lot of Toads before you find your Prince.
WOMEN LOVE THE SIMPLE THINGS IN LIFE LIKE MEN
WOMEN LOVE THE LITTLE THINGS IN LIFE LIKE MINE
women are called birds because of all the worms they pick up!
SAVE TREES -
MY BOYFRIEND IS LIKE A FAIRY TALE - GRIMM!
MEN SHOULD COME WITH A BOOK OF INSTRUCTIONS
SAY IT WITH FLOWERS GIVE HIM A TRIFFID!

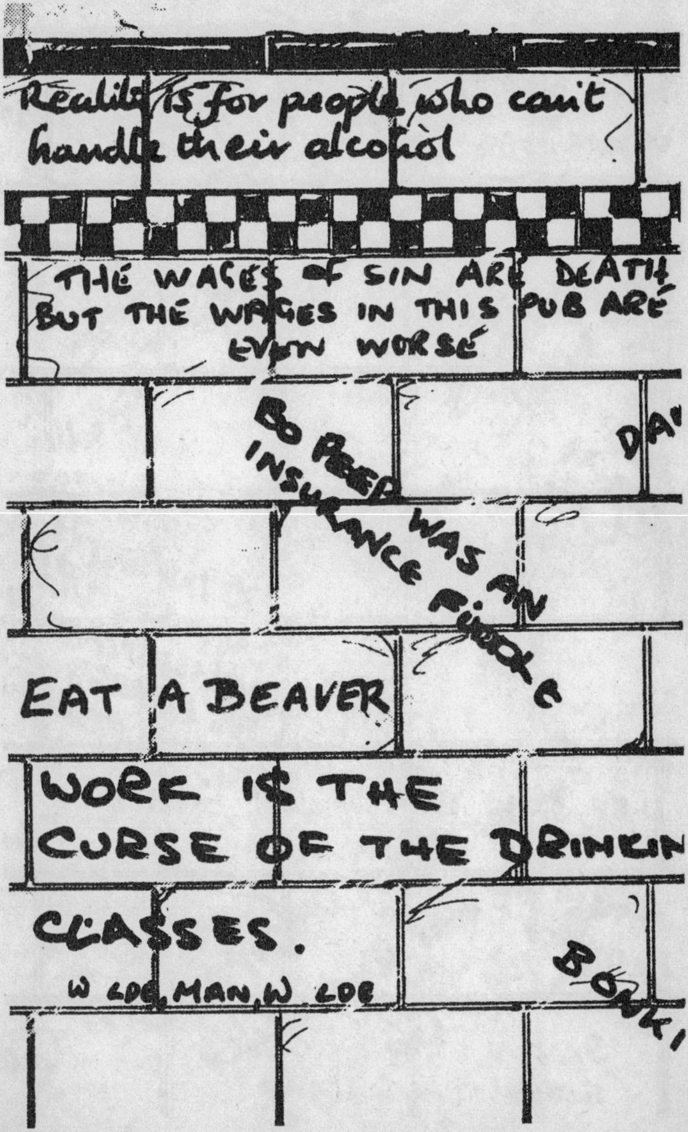
Reality is for people who can't handle their alcohol
THE WAGES OF SIN ARE DEATH BUT THE WAGES IN THIS PUB ARE EVEN WORSE
BO PEEP WAS AN
INSURANCE
EAT A BEAVER
WORK IS THE CURSE OF THE DRINKIN
CLASSES.
W LDE, MAN, W LDE
BONK

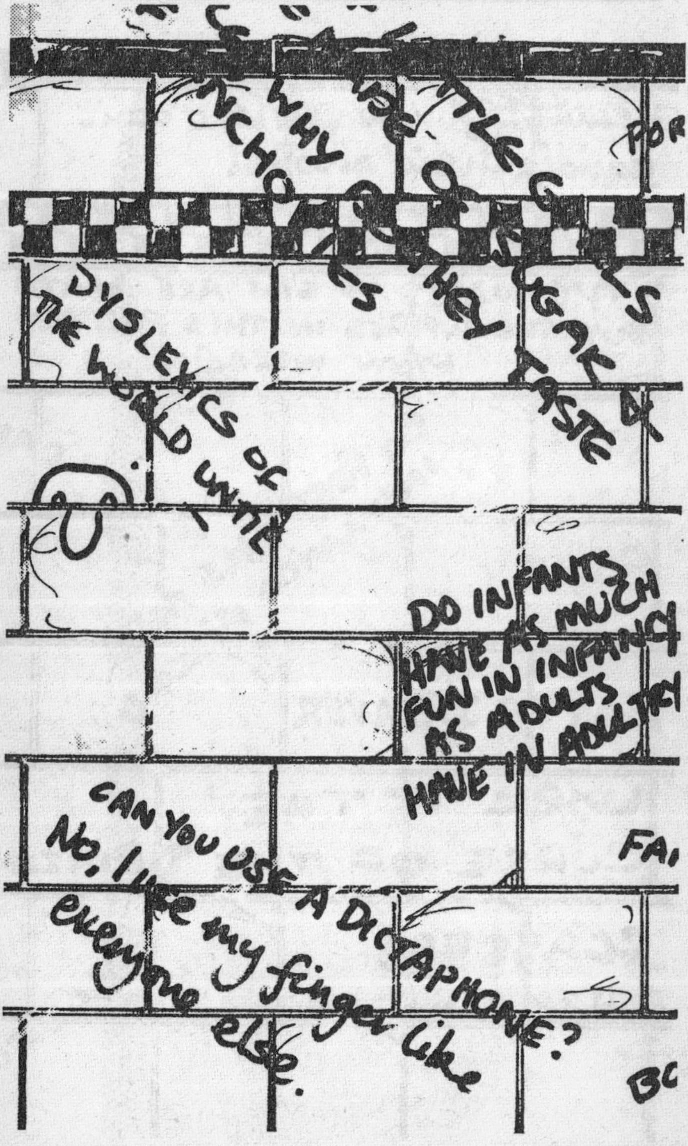
WHY
DYSLEXICS OF
THE WORLD UNTIE
DO INFANTS
HAVE AS MUCH
FUN IN INFANC
AS ADULTS
HAVE IN ADULTRY
CAN YOU USE A DICTAPHONE?
No, I use my finger like
everyone else.

BACON!
NDY!
EX
OWTH!
Brandex
SENSATIONS
THIS IS THE WORST BUBBLE GUM I'VE EVER TASTED
BUT YOU CAN BLOW SOME VERY STRANGE BUBBLES!
50P
PACK OF THREE
My mother says
these don't work!

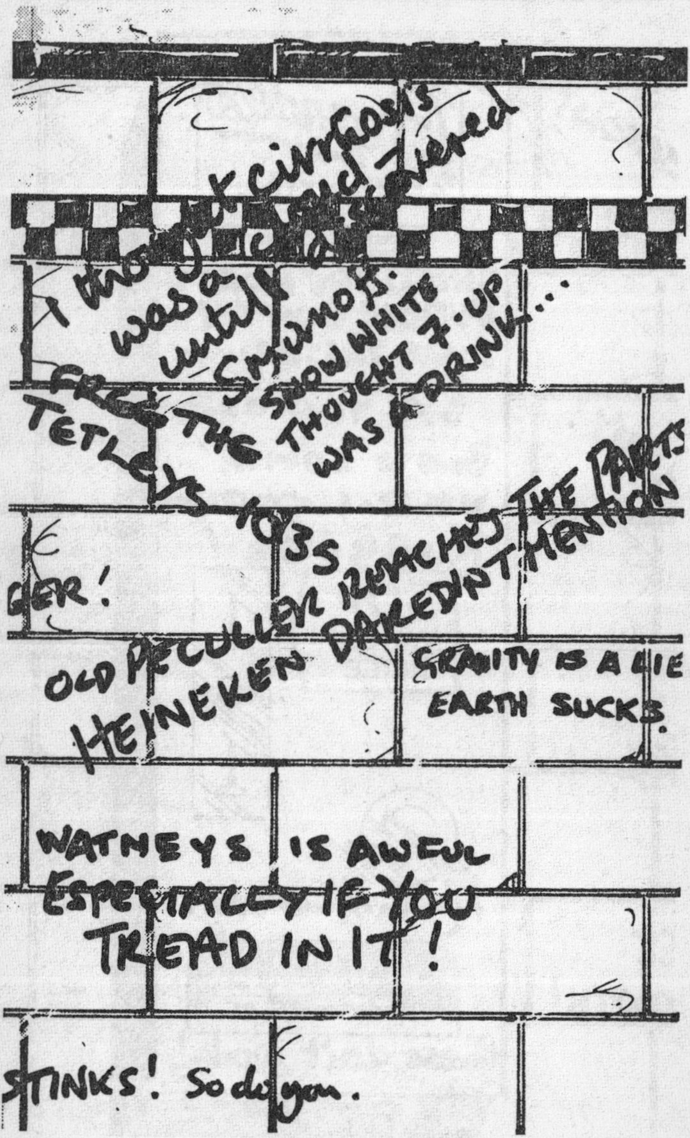
I thought cirrhosis was a tree until I discovered Smirnoff.
SNOW WHITE THOUGHT 7-UP WAS A DRINK...
FREE THE TETLEYS 1035
GER!
OLD PECULIER REACHES THE PARTS HEINEKEN DAREDNT MENTION
GRAVITY IS A LIE EARTH SUCKS.
WATNEYS IS AWFUL ESPECIALLY IF YOU TREAD IN IT!
STINKS! So do you.

Worthy winner

IT WAS panic stations at a Midland beer festival when a BBC filmcrew arrived, hoping to catch the winner of the "Birmingham's rudest landlord" competition.

The trouble was, the proud winner was not there to receive his accolade. Imagine the chagrin of publicity gal Ruth Gledhill when she hurriedly phoned to ask him along—only to be given a sharp "F... off!"

Well stoned

AN extremely fat, middle-aged bloke with his leg in plaster hobbled into his local, leaning heavily on a pair of crutches. "Blimey, Arthur," said the landlord, "what happened to you?"

"I had too much to drink at the party for my twenty-first, fell over and broke my leg."

"But your twenty-first birthday was ages ago."

"Not years, stones!"

Half and half

BREWERS Courage and Greene King may have a new drink in their pubs. Take a half of their Harp Lager, the thinking man's drink-driving specimen, and add a half of the ludicrously expensive Kronenbourg 1987. The result, I am assured by brainless oafs at my local, is called a pint of Krarp.

Kiss off

IN these permissive times of crumbling moral values, it's good to hear of pubs that remind you of the days when Ayds were just toffees for slimmers.

One such hostelry is the Woolpack at Fornham, Suffolk, a Greene King house. A Mr. and Mrs. Arkley (aged 35 and 40) were shown the red card during their lunchtime drink, when Mr. suddenly planted a peck on the cheek of his Mrs.

We all know what such cupid stunts can lead to—but in a public bar? Surely not.

This merry little jape appeared in a glossy magazine called Penthouse, which I gather is distributed free of charge to all men's hairdressing establishments. I think it is meant to imply that if you drink Barbican you acquire the ability to make farts talk.

Foaling about

THE licensee of the Waggoners, Ayot Green, Herts., will not be selling copies of the Good Beer Guide, because the comment about the pub reads: "Landlady has a lovely ass." As furious Kathy Pearce explained, she kept a donkey for years, but it has never been mentioned before.

Sniff bit

AN honest marketing slogan is about as rare as a decent pint of lager. So it is with especial pleasure that I discovered Alphafame Ltd. and their new product "Trumps".

No bull here. "Trumps are a healthy snack for husbands, wives, boyfriends, girlfriends and friends alike," starts the blurb, unpromisingly. The titbits are embued with charcoal and rose essence and they sell on the slogan. "Helps stop smelly wind."

An absorbing idea.

Boob tube

"MAKERS of a new beer called Nude," an American newspaper reports, "have had to cover the breasts of the topless model on the can because of US government protests. But drinkers who admire the feminine form will be able to 'undress' her by scratching off the ink covering. Californian William Boam, beer-with-body's innovator, plans to feature a different topless model each month."

"Of course, the drink ruined him as a stuntman."

Dad's drinkers

DURING the Second World War, the Wiltshire village of Manningford had no pub and the Home Guard used to repair to the back room of the local off-licence for refreshment.

One Sunday lunchtime, the village bobby nicked the whole platoon and the off-licence owner, cautioning them as follows: "Got you at last for illegal drinking—you're up before the beak in the morning."

To the constable's chagrin, the magistrate turned out to be the Home Guard Colonel, who declared sternly: "This disgraceful illegal drinking must stop"—and promptly awarded a full on-licence to the premises.

No beer

WATNEY MANN, whose generosity has benefitted the Conservative Party in recent years, have a permanent box at the Royal Albert Hall in London so they can invite their "friends from the Press" to free shows. The only thing missing from the box is beer, as all Watney executives prefer gin and tonic. When one intrepid Fleet Street man asked for a pint of draught, he was told: "You must be joking."

Annual bust-up?

A PUBLIC notice caught my eye: "The annual liquidation meeting of Tomatin Distillers Ltd will be held at Becket House, 1 Lambeth Palace Road, London SE1." Sounds like a nice regular do.

Fishy thought

IF a German tourist in London partakes of too much Young's or Fuller's and falls into a palace of release (better known as a bog) in a state of insobriety, would that make him a soused Herren?

Irish joke

JANE Head cooks an amazing beef and Beamish pie at her Young's pub, The Malt at Dartford, Kent.

Its fame even spread to Beamish stout headquarters in Cork where President, Richard Beamish, commanded that a portion be brought to him by Managing Director, Tony Halpin, on his next visit.

But even the best laid plans can go astray. On arrival at the Irish Customs post, the specially baked pie was spotted by an eagle-eyed officer and impounded, alongside the cocaine bricks and the Kalashnikovs.

Prolonged negotiations allowed it to pass on to Cork, provided it was accompanied by two Customs officials every step of the way.

At Beamish Palace, the hapless President was then allowed to sniff it—prior to the officers snatching it from under his nose and shoving it untouched into an incinerator.

Apparently, it is illegal to import beef into Ireland because it might cause foot and mouth disease.

True grit

THE Austrian government has always had a problem with snow. Keeping it off their roads involves pouring enormous quanties of salt around the place and come the Spring there is a flood of brine which kills off the plant life.

But this year officials remembered the millions of gallons of wine spiked with antifreeze that are still lying around the Republik. Tests have shown not only that the tainted tipple shifts snow from the autobahns but also that young plants thrive on the stuff.

Thank you, Sir – change at Newton Abbot."

Lost bottle

BEER enthusiast Mel Vaughan of Brookdale in Birmingham was ordered by a judge in the divorce court to auction off the 600 bottles from his rare beers collection in order to pay towards his divorce settlement.

But Mel went one better and arranged for an additional 100 bottles of a special beer—Mel's Heartbreak Ale—to be auctioned off as well. The proceeds from this part of the sale went to the Marriage Guidance Council.

Islay unlikely

NEIL Wilson's book *Scotch and Water* tells of the funeral in the 1860s of one John Campbell, chamberlain to the Duke of Argyll, on the peat-smoked whisky haven of Islay.

Being a remote and barren place, before the days of motorised hearses, the coffin had to be carried some distance to the kirk for burial.

Relays of pall-bearers had to make frequent stops for rest and a dram or two of recuperation on the way, but each citizen did his bit.

It was only when the graveside was reached that It was realised that Mr. Campbell and his heavy wooden overcoat were missing. Left by the wayside some miles afore.

MILES KINGTON'S LOST CAREER

Confessions of a non-wine buff

If all had gone according to plan, I would by now be one of the foremost British experts on wine. Nowadays almost everyone is expected to be on talking terms with at least a dozen varieties of grape, and nobody is surprised when someone like Auberon Waugh suddenly turns into a wine consultant; but even in such company I think I would have stood out, because my training would have been vastly superior to theirs. The only drawback was that my training never took. I was brought up to be a top wine man and it was such an unsuccessful process that I have remained one of the most cheerfully ignorant wine-tasters of my generation.

It was my father's plan. He was a director of Border Breweries in Wrexham, North Wales, which had a flourishing wine and spirits division, and he saw me eventually moving into it and learning the trade. When I opted at about 14 to specialize in languages at school, he was absolutely delighted. It wasn't the fact that I would be able to taste Voltaire and Heine at first hand that delighted him, but the thought that I could sally forth from Wrexham and talk to wine-growers in their own language.

"If all goes well, you'll be an all-purpose European buyer and seller, Miles. Whenever I go to France or Germany to do business, I'm always aware of not being able to speak the language properly, but with French, German and some Spanish, you'll be ideal. Pity about not having Italian, but you can learn that later."

For part of my summer holidays he used to send me abroad to keep learning the languages, and I almost always stayed with families connected with the drink trade. At the age of 17 I stayed in Koblenz with a nice German family and learnt about grapes before being sent on to a family in Wüppertal my father had visited before me; in 1945, as a matter of fact, as a member of the newly arrived Royal Welsh Fusiliers who had, if my father's version of the war was at all correct, won it more or less single-handed with occasional help from Churchill.

"Those of us who had any specialist knowledge were

kept behind to help get Germany on her feet again," said Dad. "Well, I was a brewer, and Wüppertal was a big brewing place, so I spent six months there working at the Wicküler Brauerei, I've written to the present head of the place, a Mr Bürgener, and he has agreed to let you stay for a while."

Mr Bürgener was a large, gruff man, a bit like President Hindenburg, and he lived in a huge, gruff house all alone except for his wife and a grown-up son called Wilfried. All Mr Bürgener wanted to do was make beer and all Wilfried wanted to do was drive round Wüppertal in a fast sports car, meeting the other rich young kids of the town, while Frau Bürgener cooked meals for both of them. Wilfried must have sighed deeply at the thought of having to chaperone a shy, 17-year-old English boy round the place, but he never let on—indeed, he was deeply impressed by the fact that I knew the German for gear lever, *Schalthebel.*

One day, Mr Bürgener took me off to the Wicküler Brauerei, which was an enormous place compared with Border Breweries in Wrexham. He was terribly proud of it, as he might well be since he had built it up in a dozen years since the war. The vats glittered and the cellars stretched gleaming for miles, not like the friendly but rather ramshackle Victorian building of Border Breweries, which might have benefitted from being devastated by the German army and rebuilt.

"Is your father's brewery so big?" demanded Herr Bürgener.

"Not half so big," I admitted.

"Does he have so many cellars?"

"Not so many."

Mr Bürgener's satisfaction at having the bigger brewery soon started to turn to complacency, whereas I began to feel indignant on behalf of my father. Had my father not come over specially at the end of the war to get this brewery started? Was it right now for Mr Bürgener to have a bigger and better brewery? I did not think so. So when he started quoting production figures at me, I started doubling them and passing them off as Border's. Did Wicküler produce 10,000 barrels a week? Then Border did 20,000, and so on. Mr Burgener's brow grew quite furrowed with the attempt to understand how a Welsh brewery half the size of his could effortlessly produce twice as much beer.

About this time my father began to transfer his ambitions to my younger brother, Stewart, who seemed to

show more willingness to learn. He packed both of us off on a holiday, in 1961, to learn something about wine by going grape-picking. Dad had got to know the Sichel family a bit, and secured two jobs for us at Château Palmer in the Bordeaux area, so Stewart and I set off on his 250cc Vespa across France, to arrive there in time for the vendange.

About Château Palmer I remember very little. A cute little château with two peacocks in the gravelly garden and an enormous kitchen where we got bread and coffee in the morning. Myself picking grapes, hopelessly lagging behind the 16-year-old girls who'd been doing it for years, and Stewart with a big wooden basket on his back taking the grapes away. Eating outdoors in the evening with the 16-year-old girls and their families, and trying to flirt with them, except they were better at that too, having done it for years. But the fact that we were working in one of the great, great vineyards of the world, and that Château Palmer 1961 is something you would now pay a fortune for —of all that I had not the faintest idea.

Now, how is that I could have had such a perfect background and grooming for a career as a man-about-drinks and made such a mess of it? How did my brother, who even went on to study brewing for a year at Heriot-Watt in Edinburgh, leave the trade to become a cameraman and a farmer, and to spend most of the 1980s not touching alcohol at all?

I really don't know the answer, nor do I feel at all upset by my ignorance. I have a sneaking sympathy with the character in Iris Murdoch's *The Sea, The Sea* who, somewhere in the first 20 pages (I couldn't get any further) says that he refuses to become educated in wine appreciation—the only result is that your standards grow higher and you pay more money to get the same pleasure. I have no envy of my friend Barlow, who is the nearest thing I know to a wine buff, the kind of man who likes to have an anonymous glass thrust in his hand and to be challenged to name it, which he normally does after those facial contortions seen otherwise only on rabbits of a nervous disposition. Recently I bought a bottle of wine for the sole purpose of challenging Barlow to name the country of origin. (Difficult: it was Wales.)

"Well," he said, pursing his lips, pushing the wine through strange internal tubes and trying to see the label, behind my back, "it's a wine from a cold country. You can tell that, because it doesn't have enough natural sweetness, so they've added up to the maximum permitted

amount of Sussreserv. That's the additive approved of by the EEC," he explained kindly.

"How can you tell they've added it?"

"You can taste it. So it's an EEC country, coldish, northernish, probably hilly. The grape is probably Müller-Thurgau.

I looked at the label. It was Müller-Thurgau.

"But I don't think it's a Germanic country. I think it's England."

How near can you get? It broke my heart to shake my head firmly, deep inside knowing he had scored a moral victory. Naming the country of origin is child's play to someone like my friend Barlow, who would much rather be asked to name the grape variety—indeed, he is now beyond that into naming the kind of container in which the wine has been matured. I have had all these things explained to me so often that I should by now be able to out-Barlow anyone, but I can't.

Is it possible to be wine-deaf, as other people are tone-deaf? I may be. I once drank a glass of Château Palmer from some wonderful mid-1960s vintage, and have to say I found it muddy and inky.

I can, though, tell a glass of good beer from a glass of bad beer. I tried a pint of something made by Whitbread called Welsh Bitter the other day, when I was feeling very thirsty in Chepstow, and it was so sublimely tasteless and boring that my thirst magically vanished after the first gulp. On the other hand, when I first went to Southwold 20 years ago and had Adnams I knew without being told that I had just encountered one of the great beers. I was drinking a pint of lemonade shandy at the Crown Hotel, I remember, and there was a peculiar taste in it. Not unpleasant, but peculiar. Eventually I identified it: hops. I had never met a beer with enough character to get its hoppy taste through a pint of shandy before, and I hardly have since, which is one of the many reasons why I have been back to Southwold on holiday every year for the past 20.

The Crown had changed dramatically last year; from a drowsy, elderly hotel into a wine bar and restaurant that London would be proud of, and I was lucky enough to gain an audience with Simon Loftus, the man who has done so much to make Adnams as famous for wine as it is for beer. He has a small room overlooking Southwold's rooftops, converted into a wine-tasting den, not unlike a cheerful laboratory, where he invited us for a canter through some of the wines he is fondest of.

It took me straight back to Border Breweries, where my

father would vanish to the sample cellar at the slightest hint that lunchtime was approaching, except that the sample cellar was deep in the earth, a simple, white-painted, vaulted room where the latest barrels were racked and waiting for the bosses to draw off a sample pint. My father's colleagues wouldn't even have recognized Simon Loftus as being a member of the same trade.

Loftus apologized for his lack of a way with words. He needn't have done. Just as a red wine gradually becomes more friendly and expansive after being uncorked, he started to be carried away by the romance of wine-making and by the stories that lay behind each bottle, until after about 20 minutes he was telling tales like an old wizard.

What was patently obvious to me was that along with all the characters he mentioned – the Professor of Viniculture at Bordeaux and his pink wine; the peasant bloke; the men from the Côtes du Rhone who came to Southwold in February and did a combined wine and apricot deal; the Burgundy grower and his American wife Pamela – Loftus himself was as much of a character. The extraordinary thing was that he could date precisely the start of his interest in wine.

"My father, who also was involved in Adnams Brewery, had a good wine cellar which was unfortunately flooded during the great east coast floods of 1953. The wine wasn't affected, but all the labels were washed off, which meant that you couldn't identify any of them. So he decided to drink his way through them over the next year, putting a name to them as he went. I remember being given a Mouton-Rothschild of some great year and being told what a great wine it was, and I can remember distinctly, although only a small boy, knowing instinctively that it was a great wine and yet at the same time that there was something badly wrong with it. It was only much later that I realized what it was – we were drinking it long before it had matured – but I am sure of this feeling that I knew, at the time, something was wrong."

I also learnt from Simon Loftus on that sunny day up in his little wine eyrie what it is that wine merchants chiefly fear and resent: the arrival of friends bearing bottles of wine they have picked up on holiday, insisting that this great discovery should be tasted. They are, said Loftus firmly, almost without exception dreadful. It was at this embarrassing point that I produced a bottle of red wine I had picked up on holiday, a Comte de Toulonnais, from the south-west, on sale at a wayside wine shrine near La Roche-Bernard in Brittany, and it says a lot for Loftus's

tolerance that he agreed to taste it. He sipped and gesticulated, spat and reflected. After a tense silence, he came out with the nearest thing to a compliment I could have hoped for: "Hmm, it has none of the expected defects." He even sent for Hugh Johnson's *Wine Atlas of the World* to look up this unknown Comte de Toulonnais and found it listed in a footnote so terse that he commented: "It's pretty clear to me that even Hugh Johnson himself hasn't tasted this one, though he doesn't admit it."

I don't suppose it ever occurred to Simon Loftus that day last July that he was helping me to exorcise a small shadow of guilt. Here, at last, was the son of a brewer who had done just what I was supposed to have done. He had become drawn into the wine world and made his small brewery famous for its wines; but far from making me feel that I should have done the same, he gives me the comforting illusion that he has done it *instead* of me. I can now go on being wine-deaf without a pang of conscience.

And if I *had* decided to go into the brewery after my father, I would now be without a job. Two years ago Border Breweries were taken over by Marston's, and the old friendly brewery, with the railway line running on a bridge across it and the red Ruabon brick chimney towering above it, was closed down. This Christmas it was set on fire, probably by homeless squatters, and is now a gutted derelict site, no longer steaming, smelling of yeast day and night, and resounding to the crash of rolling barrels. It looks just as the Wicküler Brauerei in Wüppertal must have looked in 1945, in fact, but this time I'm glad my father wasn't around to see it.

Miles Kington

Scotched

LOOKS like even discriminating television sets can't stand keg beer. Mavis Wilson runs the Crown in Spennymoor, Co. Durham, and every time a pint of fizzade is finger-tipped, the television set in the bar mysteriously changes channel.

"We can't understand it," says a perplexed Mavis. "The telly isn't linked to the beer motor. It gets a bit annoying for the racing fans. One afternoon they were following the big race but as soon as a pint of Scotch was pulled they found themselves viewing Watch with Mother."

Sheepish tale

A booklet called Cheshire Village Memories recalls:

"When the shepherds were bringing their sheep down to the lower pastures for the winter they used to call at one of the village inns [in Mellor] to refresh themselves. As they became more and more convivial the landlord and his wife were able to defraud them by giving false measure—the beer being half froth—and by chalking up too many drinks.

"One night an ominous rumbling noise came from the cellar and in great fear the landlord peered down into a pair of green eyes. 'What with thee chalkin' and me frothin', he cried to his wife, "tis the Devil come to punish us!'

"But it was only a poor ram that had fallen down into the cellar."

Old rope

ALBERT Pierrepoint, when he retired as England's greatest ever hangman, became the licensee of an inn called "Help the Poor Struggler".

Prince's Head?

THE dust, candyfloss and confetti have settled following the Royal nuptials and now the happy couple can get down to swigging the vast quantities of celebration ale brewed for them by the nation's brewers, our court correspondent, Ivor Longue-Tung reports.

The gravities of some of these ales, all dutifully supplied to Buck House, are literally and physically so staggering that one wonders if the brewers responsible had forgotten Dr. Samuel Johnston's remark that "alcohol heightens the expectation but ruins the performance".

We will draw a discreet veil over what the Prince was expected to do after consuming Wells "Cheers Charles" Wedding Ale (1060 degrees), Theakston's "Prince of Ales" (1075) and King and Barnes' "Royal Choice" with an unbelievable gravity of 1100.

Thankfully, K&B decided against calling their ale "King and Di".

Shock, horror

A YOUNG lady reporter on the Daily Mirror was accused by her harassed executives of being unable to "organise a piss-up in a brewery". Much offended, she hurried off to a nearby brewery and organised a bevvy up for her colleagues.

She handed round invitations to the slavering news hacks, who turned up mob-handed on the appropriate day—much to the consternation of the brewery hands, who had no beer to spare.

They were expecting the Mirror men the next day. The lady reporter had got the day wrong.

Angry angel

OUR legal correspondent, Ivor Ritt, writes: Great interest has been stirred in legal circles by the possibility of the first-ever example of a heavenly body suing a large public company for defamation of character.

St. Modwen, currently residing in Heaven and formerly of Burton upon Trent, has taken solicitor's advice over a major advertising campaign promoting Double Diamond, brewed by Messrs. Ind Coope, also of the parish of Burton.

St. Modwen's claim for substantial damages—believed to be a new harp and spare wings—is based on the fact that the advertisement suggests that Double Diamond is as pure and natural as the ale brewed by Modwen, who created the first monastic brewhouse in Burton.

St. Modwen told the Heavenly Times: "Suche a claym is a monstrous falsehood that should condemn yts perpetrators to everlast-

ing hell-fyre. Ye ale brewed in Burton in my tyme was wholesome and pure, whereas ye foule concoction called DD has undergone ye vyle and noxious systeme of embalming, now knowne as pasteurisation.

"It is further understoode that in place of ye sweet-smellinge herbes, rootes and plantes, ye moderne ale is rendered bittere by ye use of a Dutch weede called ye hoppe."

St. Modwen is determined to press her claim and to clear the good name of all Burton brewsters. The case is expected to come to court next year but some difficulty is expected in deciding whether it should be heard in Heaven or Hell (better known as the Skol Lager Brewery).

Holy smoke!

WHILE British brewers mess about sponsoring horse races, rock concerts and the like, their colonial cousins, South Australia Brewing Holdings, are hitting the big league.

Perhaps as part of an exercise to expand demand in the afterlife, they are sponsoring the Pope's visit to Oz.

Bright spark

FROM the Beer and Bible belt—the following note was seen scrawled beneath the new electric lighting installed in a Buckinghamshire pub's outside Gents lavatory: "I shall be a light to lighten the genitals."

Jesus wept

COLLECTORS of bad taste will be delighted to hear that the only British pub to be named after our Lord's birthplace, The Manger at Bradfield Combust in Suffolk, has opened a disco bar. The name? Christies, of course.

Church offering

WANDSWORTH brewers, Young's, have been disgracing themselves of late—or rather their mascot has.

When St. Phillip's Church in South London held a special animal blessing service, Ramrod the brewery's ram mascot, joined dogs, cats, budgies and even goldfish in the pews.

Sad to relate, Ramrod was so overcome by the atmosphere that he left what the vicar described as "a rather unholy donation" by the church door.

Bum note

I'M not sure I should be telling you this. It might cause a panic rush from the pub. But I'll risk it in the interest of the nation's health.

Are you sitting comfortably? If not you might already be a sufferer.

You see, to put it as delicately as possible, in order not to cause unnecessary embarrassment. Well, err . . . beer drinking can give you cancer of the bum.

I'm not talking about that common or garden lovely bunch of coconuts—piles. But rectal carcinoma.

According to an article in Nutrition Review, a study of 8006 men on the Hawaiian island of Oaku, revealed a link between the quantity of beer consumed and rectal cancer. Must be all that chilled and canned Budweiser.

The report also reveals that an excess of deaths from the lowest form of cancer has also been found in brewery workers in Ireland—but not Denmark.

Panic. Hallo Carlsberg. Goodbye Guinness. On second thoughts even cancer is not worth going to that length.

"Promised his wife he wouldn't touch another glass of beer as long as he lived."

VASTCO BREWERIES
THE BUSINESS REALLY BEGAN TO TAKE OFF WHEN WE STOPPED ADDING MALT, HOPS AND YEAST
LIST OF ADDITIVES
HECTOR BREEZE

AND THIS IS WHERE THE TRADITIONAL COLOURING, FLAVOURING AND PRESERVATIVES ARE ADDED
HECTOR BREEZE

Real hops?

MR. A. J. PLANT of Hornchurch in Essex sends me the following disturbing epistle:

"My father, who is an OAP, went for a trip to Leigh-on-Sea. He went into the Crooked Billet and purchased a pint of Burton Ale. Three-quarters of the way down the pint he noticed something at the bottom of the glass.

"On closer inspection he discovered that it was a dead tadpole. He then asked for the manager and received a mouthful of abuse. In fact, the manager accused him of putting the tadpole in himself, saying 'I've seen some tricks to get a free pint, but this is the best yet.'"

Mynah offence

ONE of those talking blackbirds has been barred from the lounge at a pub near Wrexham, because of its colourful language. Claude, the pet at The Plough, Isycoed, also tells people "you're getting on my nerves", wolf whistles and does useful impersonations of dog barks and vacuum cleaners.

Cardboard ale

WE are grateful to the eager eye who sent us the following cutting from the Morning Advertiser:

"Most modern beers are made from woodpulp but in the 50 years which have elapsed since these items became a regular feature of the pub environment a variety of substances have been tried. Rubber foam, plastic, cork, felt, wood, cellulose wadding, lino and paper have all had a brief vogue."

Before you sign the pledge or retire to a monastery/nunnery, be reassured. The article was on "tegestology" and a vital word was missing from the first line between "beers" and "are made". The word is "mats" . . .

Wet excuse

A WELSH pub was wrenched out of the 1981 Good Beer Guide shortly before it went to press following an urgent memo to the editor from the local branch, which ran: "The landlord of the Llareggub Arms was recently done for watering his beer. His excuse was that, while hosepiping the cellar, water somehow managed to get through the spile hole of an open-vented cask."

Inn perspective

IT'S always reassuring to return to the landlord's daily paper, our friend the "Morning Advertiser." Whatever the problems of the world, the MA immediately cuts them down to size.

The tense blockade of the Libyan People's Bureau in London was headlined: "Embassy siege hits trade at pub." Taylor Walker's Red Lion, it seems, was caught the wrong side of the police cordon in St. James's Square.

I am sure if a full-scale nuclear attack hit Britain, the MA would headline it: "Pub takings down as millions of customers die."

Pin-ups

GARDENERS should forget fertilisers and use Draught Bass; that's the word of horticultural wisdom from the Exeter Arms Hotel, at Middlemoor, Exeter. The Hotel boasts a bank of eight monster-sized sunflowers, all raised on real ale. Said the manager: "They do tend to fall over if they have a bit too much—that's why they are nailed to the wall."

"OK to bring the dog in?"

"I've been thinking, Mildred. Do we ***really*** *need a bouncer?"*

On being excluded from the Guide

We've just been drummed out of the Brownies,
Removed from the beer drinkers guide.
The ultimate humiliation,
Our faces in shame we must hide.

Does this mean we'll get no more visits,
From serious young men in flared jeans?
Who demand to know what the O.G. is,
Though they're not really sure what it means.

No more groups in obscure brewery tee-shirts,
Tightly clutching their half pints of beer.
First a sniff—then a sip—then a swallow,
After making quite certain it's clear.

What can we have done to offend them?
These self proclaimed experts on booze.
Just what are the things that they look for,
When deciding which pubs they will choose?

Perhaps we should alter our image,
And serve Chilli and Curry 'til ten.
Maybe then we would get reinstated,
Back in the Good 'Beer' Guide again.

Or we could add some instant nostalgia,
Put up shelves filled with old books and pots.
And cover the walls in old pictures,
Bought at a sale in job lots.

Or maybe we'll choose to ignore them,
And try to put on a brave face.
For it's probably not too important,
We've a feeling that could be the case.

Anon.

WITHIN PUB WALLS ~ A LOCAL ANALYSIS
FIRST A PINT ..... BUT WHERE'S THE BAR?
THUNK!
BOOM
..DO YOU KNOCK TO ASK...
..CALCULATE YOUR TRAJECTORY
...OR FOLLOW THE CROWD?
ARE ALL EYES ON ...?
OH WHAT A GOAL!
BZZZZ
A-A-R-G-H!
..THE BRAND NEW TELE...
..AQUARIUM ACTIVITIES
..THE McAWFUL'S KEG DRINKER?
WHAT HAPPY GROUP TO JOIN ...?
A NUTTY LITTLE BEER!
OH YES
HMM! NOT BAD...
THUNK!
..A FLOCK OF YOUNG SOLICITORS...
..THE RUGBY HEROES..
..OR THE TEAM'S VITAL GAME?

A BRIEF INTERLOO-DE DEMANDS...?
PIRATES
BUOYS ONLY
CORDON BLEU ~ ROOM ~
MERMAIDS
..A CROSSWORD PUZZLE BRAIN..
..THE LACK OF ONE..
..OR A SENSE OF ADVENTURE?
BACK AT BASE.... YOUR PINT HAS STRAYED!
..WAS IT THE ANTIQUE COLLECTOR..
..THE GENTLE GIANT...
..OR AN OVERSIGHT?
HAS THE LANDLORD MADE YOUR NIGHT...?
ON YER BIKES!
..BY PULLING HIS WEIGHT...
..HAVING A SOCIAL WHIRL..
..OR ARRIVING JUST IN TIME?
..TIME..PLEASE!!

ALAN
COREN

Trapped behind the lounge bar

YOU KNOW why they dream it? They dream it because it is the only dream left with an outside chance. It is the only dream wherein the seriated decades do not loom like hurdles to smash your shins and scatter your teeth among the cinders.

At twenty, you recognise you will not win the Newdigate and stroke the Oxford shell through Hammersmith; at thirty, a small voice whispers that it is too late to take Joe Frazier in the third or baritone La Scala to its grateful knees; at forty, it is borne in upon you that you will neither charge the Russian guns nor, just as single-handedly, shatter the sexual taboos of Melanesia; by fifty, you have ceased to dream even of becoming Deputy Leader of the Labour Party or finding a gas lighter that works two days running.

But the dream of, someday, running a pub, shines on untarnished, like a good deed in a naughty world.

It is a good dream because it contains all the others: it is a fantasy that embraces power, pleasure, self-sufficiency, sexual possibility, money, notoriety, and social success. Great men will come whimpering to your door at 5.25, but their pleas shall not avail them. Beautiful women will beg to stay, at 11.15, and you will cast them into the night. You will subsidise this alcoholic poet, but not that; you will offer your authoritative advice to this adulterous bishop, but to his archiepiscopal sidekick you will curl the lip and ban the bottle; you will ignore the clamouring Chief Superintendent and his good lady, and serve the Hell's Angel and the Rastafarian first, you will tell the Prime Minister's husband he has had enough, you will stop Welshmen singing and kick out the millionaire's dog.

And nobody will be able to touch you, because you are the Landlord. You run the bridge, you preside over the bench, you command the army, you captain the team, you chair the board, you lead the pack and if the messiah comes again and wants a pink gin, you will draw His attention to the sign that says *Please Do Not Ask For Credit Since A Refusal Often Offends.* You dream all this. And then they let you run one:

I DID NOT, when I embarked upon this appalling exercise, have any clearly defined idea of the type of landlord I should be; rather, I felt vaguely that I might somehow emerge as a sort of glamorous cobbling of pre-formed publican images. By Surtees or Dickens, perhaps, out of John Ford and the *New Yorker*; a rubicund, jolly, spiritually side-whiskered cove, an MFH and randy JP, say, who for all his bucolic bonhomie keeps a dog-leg Colt .45 within easy reach beneath the bar in the event of the James boys getting fresh with the Ladies' Darts Team or of Ike Clanton coming for his boy after I have leapt the bar and thrashed him within an inch of his life for dealing his dominoes from the bottom of the deck—yet, at the same time, a taciturn man in a made-up bow, prepared to stand for hours in silence, slowly wiping the same whisk(e)y glass and ostensibly listening while a sharp-suited media executive weepingly describes his impotence or a vomit-blotched hack from *The Spectator* goes on and on and on about the rotten novel he might one day get around to writing.

That I was called upon to fulfil none of these functions may come as scant surprise to those who know Watford. Lovely though Watford undeniably is, it is neither W.53rd Street nor Tombstone, and the Quorn is an infrequent visitor, unless a fox turns the wrong way onto the M1. Watford thus has different priorities.

"There's half-eaten sausages all over the garden," said Dickinson, lurching past me, purple-faced, during the

lunchtime miasma, bearing lunches nos. 73 to 77 between hatch and the impatient tablesful of eaters waiting out back, beneath the trees. He had mustard in his hair. "Look at these shoes!" The hatch being at one end of the narrow bar and the garden door being at the other, Dickinson was required to squeeze by me and the open till, perhaps as good a method as any of introducing onions into the two-bob tray.

"What?" I said. It is only a small word, but it is enough to demolish the finely-wrought structures the brain can carry, such as the change out of a tenner for a large gin and low-calorie tonic, a whisky mac, a light-and-bitter in a thin glass, a pint of lager in a tankard, a half-pint of lager with blackcurrant (sic), and one of them new things. I don't know, son, you're the bleeding barman, it was on the telly, there's that big bloke that drinks it, it's got sort of a bee on the label or am I thinking of that soup, anyway one of them, and a packet of mixed nuts, provided there's no cashews in it.

But Dickinson did not stay for a reply, bound as he was to the lunchtime wheel of fire, doomed like the Chaplin of *Modern Times* to be forever one step behind the unending stream of plates whizzing up from the kitchen; the pitiful soul struggled gamely on beneath his burden of rolls and pasties and battered cods, through the swing door which, as it banged back into place, batted a dropped cheese sandwich past me on the half-volley, into the scummy spillage that threatened at any moment to engulf the welt. I feared for the diminutive genius; geriatric readers of these lines may well recall where Dickinson and I have been together; we have nearly swum the Channel, we have to all intents and purposes conquered the Swiss Alps, we have hunted lion and wildebeest, albeit in Wilts; it is probably no exaggeration to say that we are perhaps the Hinge and Bracket of investigative journalism, and in all these the plucky mite has served with fortitude and élan. To see him reduced to ruin by Watford's lunchers wrenched the heart.

Not that I had unthinkingly consigned him to the hell of waiting. I had tried him behind the bar, but it had been disastrous. How odd that one can be close to another human being for half a lifetime, and never realise that it cannot count! I know about Dickinson's ailments, I know about his children's aspirations and his cat's funny little ways; I know about the trouble he has finding trousers and barbers; I have heard a great deal about the peculiar noise in his Metro, and yet I have been given no inkling of the fact that if you ask Dickinson to add the price of a French vermouth (57p) to the price of a pint of cooking bitter (69p) his eyes glaze and he begins to tremble uncontrollably.

That is bad news when you are behind a bar, facing outwards. It is a strange, and totally unanticipated, sensation: serried rows of mouths, bobbing slightly, jockeying for position and attention, and never going away. The barman finds himself in the position of a mother sparrow, gullets fill the horizon, tonsils glow and wobble, you keep on filling them up, and still the bastards come,

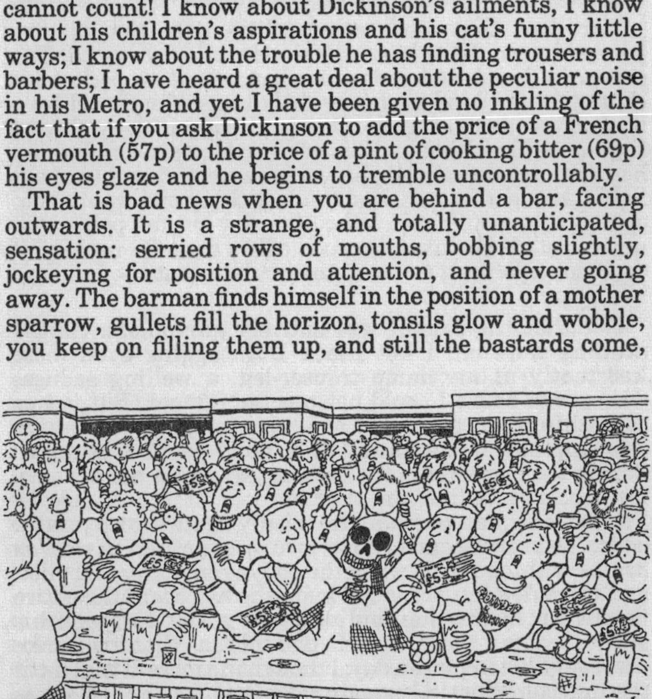

the pints go down, the front row eases out, the second row steps forward; it is Waterloo, it is Rorke's Drift, and by the time the fifth row has been filled to the brim, the first row is back from the gents and ready for topping up again. It is a great unending liquid cycle, magnificent in its own peculiar way, and unquestionably horrible.

It follows from this that it is somewhat tricky to be both accurate and civil. The dream of chewing the fat with the more engaging locals, which sustains so many pub-aspirants, becomes in fact a nightmare: in the course of an evening of rapid calculations that would melt down any IBM product currently on the market, you are carefully holding in your head a multiple order for fourteen mixed drinks and poised, finally, to punch the myriad and complex numbers into the till, and some fool leans across the bar and says, "I see Willis took five for ninety-seven," the natural inclination is to break a siphon over his head.

Nor does that other conviviality-myth, the one-for-yourself, turn out to have any worthwhile substance. One comes to dread that moment when, about to pocket his change, some kind customer feels himself suffused by a flush of goodwill or guilt. One is already cock-eyed from the fumes breathing up from one's sodden sleeves; half an hour's simple inhaling behind a bar is equivalent to about half a bottle of scotch, and the last thing one wants is to open one's mouth and infect the few pitiful pores still unsaturated. Fortunately, such offers dwindle rapidly; it does not take long for word to circulate that the landlord is a gloomy bastard.

Not that the canard was entirely groundless. As the evening wore on, I felt Black Dog tugging even more insistently at my damp trouser-leg, a welling sadness whose root cause I could not precisely finger. But it was something to do with the spectacle of obsessive consumption, underpinned by a truly terrible statistic: during the epicentre of the evening, when the bar became, for me, not unlike the engine-room of the foundered *Titanic,* one man pumping frenziedly against insuperable odds, the brain began to go its own wool-gathering way, as brains will tend to do when the body is on automatic pilot, and I recalled the words of a man who had spent the entire lunchtime in the pub and was now about to spend his entire evening there, too. He had told me that his intake was roughly ten pints a day; I thought no more of that until the unfettered brain began to calculate. Ten pints a day is getting on for five hundred gallons a year, and if the drinking lifetime is on average fifty years, this man by the time he is seventy will have drunk around 25,000 gallons of beer. This works out, as the brain clunked and whirred and drew on those tiny figures in the front of diaries long ago, at a little over four thousand cubic feet. An oblong 50 feet long by 20 feet wide, 3 feet deep at one end and grading to 6 feet deep at the other.

This man will have drunk a municipal swimming-pool full of Benskins bitter. At current prices, it will have cost him £140,000.

"What's up?" said Dickinson, ever sensitive to the shifting clouds on his master's face. I told him.

He took out a pedometer. "So what?" he said. "I have walked 13·2 miles today."

"It does not cheer me up," I said. "All it means is that if that man wants to drink 25,000 gallons in fifty years at a cost of £140,000, you will have to walk 240,900 miles to help him do it. That is the exact distance to the Moon."

We stared at one another across this fearful statistical pit. *"Get on with it!"* screamed the patrons.

I should quickly point out that there is a way of offsetting some of the beastliness. I have long held the principle, with no thought of my own safety, that the only way to avoid these problems of sexual harassment which seem to beset the modern office is to employ female staff of such stunning quality that no man on the premises would have the temerity to throw a pass at it, recognising that our women clearly have the pick of the world's sheikhs, royals, and lead guitarists. Wisely, Dickinson and I shipped two of these paragons out to Watford with us, so that if the local clientele ever went past the point of sufference with our ineptitude, we could bang in as reserves a brace of barmaids that would knock their socks off.

As theory, it was irreproachable. In practice, it worked

so well that our brave little team was lucky to get out alive.

There are no images conveniently to hand to describe the exact effect, at nine o'clock on that seething summer evening, of firing Catherine and Dorothy off the trainer's bench. One recalls the Lord's pitch explosion after the World Cup Final, for example, when most of Southall advanced shrieking on Kapil Dev; one remembers the lunge at Wodge, I believe it is pronounced, or possibly the wodge at Lunge, when getting on for upteem million Poles surged towards HH the P; yet these were as naught compared with what gripped the drinkers of Watford when our voluptuous substitutes rose from behind the sodden bar like Botticelli clones

It was a poignant moment, in its own coarse way. Two Fay Wrays and a scrum of King Kongs, the great simple animals strangely stirred at faint atavistic memories of

the days before the only thing worth living for came out of casks. One sensed a sort of, how shall I put it, a sort of yearning, some might say a need, a deeply moving nympholepsy.

"Bloody hellfire," muttered Dickinson, at our now-deserted end of the bar, "there is clearly not a lot of it available in Watford."

"Oh, I don't know," I said, since, among other things, I didn't. "Are we not here looking at yet another heartrending example of men committed to the pursuit of fantasy? Does it not share something with our own touching dream of landlordship?"

My pot-boy stared blankly at me from beneath his beer-plastered fringe.

"Let's go and pick up the bloody sausages," he said.

Alan Coren

SORRY! NO MOTOR BIKE GEAR, CRASH HELMETS. LEATHER

IT MAKES YOU THINK

Peck of life

AFTER quenching the fire which had extensively damaged the Lamb & Flag in Swindon, firemen turned their attention to weightier matters.

While rescuing landlord Richard Walterman's two pet budgies—Billy and (would you believe) Smokie—from the towering inferno, one of the heroic hosers noticed they were turning blue at the beaks.

Whipping off his breathing apparatus he used his oxygen mask to apply the peck of life.

Saloon bar

THERE'S no answer to that letter to CAMRA HQ: "I can only enjoy drinking a good pint in a smoke-free atmosphere, and wonder if you know of any public houses with a non-smokers' room in the West Midlands. At present we usually drink in the car in the public house car park but it gets cold in winter."

Yorkshire pud

IT'S only a thought, but if a pub in a famous Yorkshire beauty spot sold only keg beer from nasty plastic boxes, would it be a case of Ilkley Moor bar tat?

"A pint of the usual, Bert."

Consumer response

WHEN the plans for modernising the Clifton Arms at Caterham, Surrey, were being drawn up, it is obvious that local drinkers were not consulted.

In retrospect this might have been a good idea as one customer, Mr Lindsey Harmon, expressed his feelings on the matter by carving out a four-foot by three-foot hole in the wall, using a chain-saw. It appears that that he felt an archway was required in the new wall.

Buried pleasure

PUBLICAN magazine ran a competition asking for suggestions for items to be buried in a "Time Capsule" at Lang's Glengoyne Distillery in Scotland. The nine artefacts were supposed to sum up the British local.

Top of the poll came a price list (really?) with a bar food menu in second place. A handpump and a copy of the Good Beer Guide were among the items landlords want buried . . . but there won't be a keg fount.

Video tapes of two of the country's most famous TV pubs, Coronation Street's Rovers Return and Emmerdale Farm's Woolpack, will also be consigned to future history.

One licensee even wanted to bury a customer—though which one he didn't specify.

The concept of summing up the British pub in a few items caught the imagination of columnist Keith Waterhouse of the Daily Mirror. His choices, perhaps, more accurately capture the spirit of the pub in the late Eighties:

"Were I asked to make up my own time capsule I

would not be so unjust as to nominate a landlord—how to choose but one out of so many candidates for incarceration?

But I would include a space-invaders table, an electronically oscillating fruit machine, a juke box, a jammed cigarette machine, an empty ice bucket, a plastic table with one leg shorter than the others, an ashtray full of crumpled crisp packets, a carpet tile that looks like a pizza, a pizza that tastes like a carpet tile, a selection of offensive, whining or joshing notices, a clock fifteen minutes fast, a strident bell, a section of eggbox-style lowered ceiling, a strobe light, a sealed-up corner door, and 20 pence in coins to represent what some of them charge for a splash of soda."

Exploding pigs

ODD experiments are being carried out on defenceless porkers down in Kent by Shepherd Neame.

The staple fare for pigs is soya bean meal, but pig farmers and the brewery have discovered that some of the by-products of the brewing process are richer in nutrient value.

As a result, unsuspecting pigs have been trotting up to their troughs, snuffling with pleasure at the thought of a quick bellyful of soya bean, to discover instead that they have been doled out a substance called "cask bottoms", which is the beery deposit left behind when we guzzling mortals have sunk the contents of a barrel.

Mind you, the amiable porkers don't seem too muffed by the new diet. On a hot day, a pig has been seen to put away a gallon of the murky stuff with no obvious ill effects. "They do look a bit drunk," said production director Colin Neame, "but pigs tend to get sleepy and not violent when they're drunk." There's a moral in that somewhere.

Shepherd Neame have also been offering yeast to pig farmers. The fermenting agent is naturally high in nutrient when it leaves the brewery but it has done some of the hapless pigs no good at all. Unless you kill the yeast cells with propionic acid, it continues to multiply and a few pigs have actually exploded due to fermentation occuring after ingestion.

What was that about pigs might fly . . . ?

PORKY & BEST: In Bradford there really is a brewery called Trough, producing Wild Boar Bitter, while Gloucestershire boasts Old Spot from the Uley Brewery

Pure venom

THE gentle jokers at Guinness love a merry jape. Like the gentleman who got fed up with staring at their ten-feet by fifty-feet advertising placard on Westminster Bridge Road.

"Fill in and send us this form to win a year's free Guinness," it said. So he did. With a chainsaw. All 100 square feet of it, hoarding and all.

A spokesman for Guinness has indicated that they would like him to come forward to claim his reward. They want to nick him for criminal damage.

Heavy weather

COURAGE have been having problems with their poster hoardings. Just 100 yards from their headquarters in Southwark a massive advertising placard was blown to the ground with a thud, nearly crushing a nearby bus shelter. "It ain't heavy, it's Miller Lite," read the slogan.

The Pils war is turning vicious. And crude. This label (read it carefully) appeared in a trade advert from (obviously worried) brand leaders, Holsten, under the heading: "Isn't it time you told all those fake Pils what to do?"

Hairy stuff

THE ultimate in clean-tasting lagers has been banned in Germany.

A court in Baden-Wurttemberg has ruled that beer-shampoo cannot be sold in bottles which could be mistaken for beer, since drunks or foreigners (and especially drunk foreigners) might knock back the hairy stuff in error.

According to European Chemical News (believed to be a Brewers' Society publication): "Research has shown that a third of all shampoo drinkers suffer either nausea, vomiting, flatulence or diarrhoea. There is also the danger that the shampoo could foam in the stomach or oesophagus and block the passage of air to the lungs."

The court found these risks too much to swallow.

Ear for beer

A RIVAL publication "for lovers of real beer" has started up in the States—called "Listen to your Beer", with pictures of drinkers lowering their ears to their glasses. Must be the snap, crackle and pop of all those taste-the-same American canned lagers.

Slug pub

SUPPORT for CAMRA has come from an unexpected quarter—the common garden slug. A firm called Pelco Products is marketing a device that turns beer into a pest killer.

The device, known as the Slug Pub, is filled with beer and left in the garden. The yeast in the beer lures the unsuspecting slugs, which topple into the vessel and drown, poor things.

In tests carried out by Pelco, Guinness and Theakston's Best Bitter proved to be the most effective slug killers. Lager, apparently, was a complete flop. It seems that, just like beer drinkers, there are discriminating slugs around.

Golden river

I'M grateful to Publican magazine for the description of drinking standard British lagers given them by an (unnamed) director of a well-known regional brewery: "Like swimming down the Thames with a hop in your mouth . . ."

Lager bar

WHILE in an Orwellian vein we were struck by the following from a new biography of George Orwell by Peter Lewis:

"His frequent appeals to 'common decency' were appeals to what he saw as working-class virtues—hard work, fair dealing, thrift, endurance, and cheap and common pleasures which he shared himself—fishing, vegetable growing, home carpentry, strong tea, strong tobacco and dark beer. He always rolled his own cigarettes and he refused to buy lager for anyone, even women."

"It's no use," said his wife, Eileen. "As a friend of his you become the kind of person who wouldn't drink lager."

Clearly, a man before his time.

A dog's life

GNASHER Rantzen's increasingly bizarre telly show *"That's Life"* got all het-up and excited when it discovered a Shropshire dog that could tell the difference between real ale and keg.

"What a wheeze," shrieked the Gnasher's team, "to present the dog with a CAMRA membership card."

Obligingly, local organiser Barry Malone and other Campaign worthies, turned up at the Last Inn, Hengoed, on the appointed day.

Our Barry, being a good CAMRA pro, carefully made sure that he imbibed no more than two pints of Wood's ale all day so that he was sober when the big moment came, and he had to hand over the Campaign gong to landlord Jim Heaton's dog, Ben. (Ben was getting the award, according to the That's Life scriptwriter for "dogged persistence in the real ale cause"—geddit?).

Only snag was that Ben did not match B. Malone's sobriety. Come the big moment, after several dozen run-throughs and with lights blazing and cameras rolling . . . the canine CAMRA-ite obligingly rolled over and went to sleep, totally pawless.

Apparently Ben had already imbibed some four pints of ale in the cause of duty. The That's Life team had to parade the dog round the icy car park for an hour or two in order to wake him up for a re-take.

Cam-a-lot

IF imitation is the sincerest form of flattery (and not just ripping off a good idea), then CAMRA should be well satisfied.

But now I am not so sure. For after the predictable campaigns for real bread, cheese and sausages—a weirder bunch of CAM-nickers has appeared.

Most alarming is the campaign for "real balls". Before sensitive gentlemen start adjusting their dress, I should explain that the idea came from the secretary of the Dartington Squash Rackets Club in Devon, who prefers the black ball when on court.

"Just as in the pubs the more discriminating prefer Real Ale, so on the squash courts the more discriminating players prefer to serve Real Ball," he claimed. Quite.

Amen corner

ANOTHER body to copy CAMRA, you will be surprised to hear, is the Prayer Book Society.

According to Yorkshire clergymen, Peter Mullen, the Society is fighting like CAMRA against a keg product—the Alternative Service Book introduced in 1908. The Society prefers the traditional Book of Common Prayer "to the fizzy and sterile" new volume.

Obviously, this bland new product is being forced on unwilling congregations by the "Big Bishops". Let us pray for the Campaign's success.

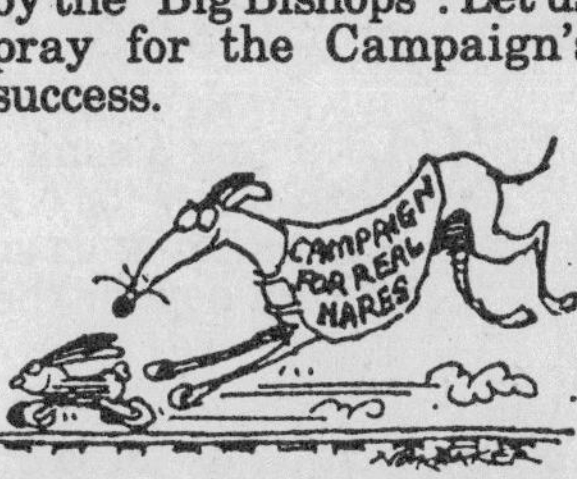

Even race-track greyhounds are getting in on the act, according to this hare-brained cartoon.

With a hey for the nut-brown ale

Let's sing a song to the pubs of the land,
With a hey for the nut-brown ale;
The blowsy, the bleary, the brash and the bland
With a hey for the nut-brown ale.

If they sell good beer in Haslemere
And under Guildford hill—
As Belloc thought eighty years ago, and
As one or two think still—
It must be the pubs they serve it in
That make you so horribly ill.

The trouble is, they've lost their function
And, with it, their geniality;
They offer what they call 'entertainment'
And never mind 'hospitality';
They only aspire to the white-walled-tyre
And Barratt House mentality.

'The Quiet Woman', 'The Plough', 'King's Arms',
'The Bull', 'The Stilton Cheese'—
England's history is enshrined
In pubs with names like these:
But 'The Doctor Who' and 'The Nickel and Dime'
Are a form of Dutch Pub Disease.

Let's sing a song to the pubs we love best
With a hey for the nut-brown ale;
As charming as sniffing a second-hand vest,
With a hey for the nut-brown ale.

Theme-pubs are the latest thing
To be thrust on us these days;
A fifth-rate panto set begotten
By a moron on a maze;
As cheap and repetitious as
A comedian's catch-phrase.

You know 'Ye Smuggler's Cave' will be full
Of polystyrene sloops,
A plastic net with a plastic lobster
Caught in its plastic loops;
Where you sit on plastic casks and drink
Warm Watneys from plastic stoups.

The loos in these theme-pubs aren't Ladies and Gents
But Cocks and Hens, Stallions and Mares,
Kings and Queens—confusing if
It catches you unawares,
And responsible for bladderwrack
In a number of foreign au pairs.

Let's sing a song to the pubs we know well
With a hey for the nut-brown ale;
A dismal and Disneyland vision of hell
With a hey for the nut-brown ale.

Even the local pub, although
It might not go quite that far,
Likes its bit of wrought-iron and glass,
Its plastic veneer on the bar,
And a clientele that never has
A pint, but always 'a jar'.

There's wipe-clean moquette all over the place
In purple and black and green;
Piped Herb Alpert, plus juke-box,
Plus 60 inch TV screen;
And if you ask for a Guinness, it comes
With a cherry and grenadine.

The barman caricatures his breed
By calling everyone 'squire';
The barmaid's warmth is slightly less
Than that from the false log-fire;
There's the sickly, suggestive, second-hand smell
Of a distant deep-fat frier.

Let's sing a song to the pubs that we loath
With a hey for the nut-brown ale.
Where the lampshades are red and the carpet
is mauve,
With a hey for the nut-brown ale

The flame-effect bulbs flicker and
The plastic Tudor creaks,
Unheard through Tijuana Brass
And juke-box-mangled shrieks;
A background roar that will ensure
That no one actually speaks.

There's no taste to the furnishings
And less taste to the beer;
The blankness on the faces, sadly,
Isn't just veneer;
The place is packed with bodies, but
There's really no one here.

So let's sing this song for the pubs of the land
With a hey for the nut-brown ale;
To all who are making a last kitsch stand
Sing hey for the nut-brown ale.

Nigel Forde

A Round at the Radcliffe Road end

EVERY SUMMER, come rain or come hail, a group of CAMRA stalwarts meets at the Radcliffe Road end of Trent Bridge cricket ground to watch either the Saturday of the Test or a one-day pyjama match. Over the years the group—the collective noun for which is "a round"—admits that there has never been a good day's cricket.

The sport has been dull, predictable or rained off; on one Saturday of appalling tedium the event was enlivened only by Ian Botham losing his temper with the umpire. But the Saturdays have all been remarkable for one thing: the quality of the beer, even when supped from a plastic glass under the stand as the heavens emptied on Nottingham.

The organising genius behind the annual gathering is Richard Sanders, who cannot for much longer be denied his rightful honour of Freeman of the Borough of Loughborough. Sanders not only buys the block of tickets but, equally important, provides the ale for the morning session before we depart to the nearest pub. His instructions to the rest of us are benignly simple: "Bring a glass".

Now Trent Bridge, in common with all cricket grounds these days, is awash with notices admonishing spectators against bringing alcohol into the ground. The assumption is that we will put up with the expensive fizzy swill sold within its walls. The idea is anathema to self-respecting CAMRA members and, from personal observation, to most of the others who attend the Radcliffe Road end.

Sanders gets round the by-laws by arriving, whatever the weather, in the type of gargantuan raincoat perfected by the in-mates of Stalag Luft 19 in the Second World War who, when building their escape tunnels, hid the extraneous sand in special pockets concealed inside the coat. When Sanders waddles to his seat he unbuttons the coat to reveal a gallon carry-keg of the finest local ale.

With words of praise ringing in his ears, Sanders fills our parade of glasses and then goes through his annual ritual of "You'll never guess what it is". Dutifully playing along, we take a few sips then cry in unison: "It's bloody Pedigree again, Richard!"

By lunchtime the carry-keg has been drained and Phase Two of the day comes into play: we go to the pub to fill both ourselves and the carry-keg in order to survive the long afternoon and evening sessions. Usually it's the Norfolk Arms for Home Bitter. It costs 76p a pint and Sanders grumbles about the high price while the southerners struggle to understand how they have got so much change for a round.

Back at the ground the Round has attempted to enliven the proceedings with a collective wit fuelled by the considerable consumption of Pedigree and Home Bitter. One year we spent the morning barracking the hapless Derek Pringle every time he laid hand on ball in the field. As we rose for luncheon in the Norfolk, a man dressed in immaculate blazer, flannels and cravat approached us with a well-honed smile and said: "May I introduce myself?" "Of course," we chorused. "I am," he said, "Derek Pringle's father."

He probably wasn't—the real Pringle Senior would surely not have been at the Radcliffe Road end—but it has curbed our behaviour a trifle. Salt was rubbed into that particular wound when Pringle Junior was named Man of the Match. I think he held a catch.

Sanders' style is less penetrating but no less effective. A couple of years ago New Zealand were grinding the English bowling so efficiently that Bracewell, chosen for his spinning abilities, scored a century. As he neared his ton, he hoisted Philippe Edmonds for six over long off at our end. Long off, inappropriately placed, was Gladstone Small, who jumped, stuck his arm up but was several inches below the ball. Sanders, seated behind me, leaned forward and said in his lugubrious East Midlands voice: "Y'know, me duck, if he had a neck, he'd have caught that."

1987 was not a vintage year. Sanders was unable to buy his usual block of tickets due to the demand for the England–Pakistan one-day game. We were divided into two groups: those with Sanders (and carry-keg); and those without Sanders (or sustenance). It was a bitterly cold day and the morning's cricket was not only dull, apart from a brief sally by Broad, but also unnaturally dry for those of us deprived of Sanders. He arrived just before lunch, his apologies undermined by his rubicund expression and beer breath, and offered to buy the first round in the Norfolk.

Such a rare and world-shattering event was not to be passed up. Safely ensconced in the lounge, we had just embarked on our third pints when someone called out: "Botham's in!" One of the Round was interrupted in mid-

Not much of a match is it?

orgy. He was holding up his glass, glorying in the skill of a master brewer, the tawny brilliance of the liquid and the need to savour such nectar with true deference when the rest of the Round emptied their glasses down their throats in one collective swallow and headed for the door.

Panting, groaning, waddling and puffing, we made our ignominious way back to the ground to catch the master in his pomp. As we crashed into our seats the scoreboard mockingly told us we should have stayed in the Norfolk. Botham had been dismissed for a great, fat blobberooni, attempting unsuccessfully to hoist the Pakistani spinner into the River Trent. Would you waste a pint of Home Bitter to watch John Emburey bat?

Roger Protz

The KINGS HEAD IN ONE
THAT PUTS THE PRESSURE ON A BIT, EH?

Gone to the lap dogs

THE lady publican of a Wadworth's tied house in Wiltshire contacted the brewery with a request to change the name of her house, the Railway Tavern. The landlady, a dedicated raiser of pedigree dogs, told Waddies that a more attractive title was required.

"Good idea," said the friendly Waddies people, and left it to her to change the name to something more suitable, like the Rose and Crown or Avebury Ring. The brewery thought no more about it until a member of the Devizes staff drove past the pub a few weeks later, and arrived at the brewery white of face and in need of a swift half of Old Timer.

The pub had changed both its name and its livery. It had been painted a shocking pink and the new inn sign depicted a Cadbury-coloured canine beast with the legend the "Chocolate Poodle".

Deceptive titles

WHAT'S in a name? Not a lot judging by a list of unwanted companies Guinness have been winding up. Among them were Meadow Irish Meats Ltd (which made mineral waters) and Boating Holidays International (who, of course, ran a pharmaceutical unit). Best of all: Harp Lager Brewery (South)—"nature of business: previously operated a cinema."

Bolton wonders

BOLTON'S drinkers are revolting. They are, in fact, forming themselves into CARPET—the Campaign for Real Pub Titles. (Yes I know it doesn't spell Carpet, and **you** know it too, but we don't come from Bolton.)

It started when the Fleece changed its name, amidst sniggers, to "The Gaiety". When that appeared to put customers off, it was altered to "Maxim's". Presumably Bolton is twinned with chic inner city Paris.

The Gypsy's Tent became "Winstons", after the cigarette of that name, the Nag's Head "Olivers" in memory of an obscure cheese biscuit, and the already idiotic "Loose Goose" waddled over the edge to become "Rosie O'Grady's Good Time Emporium".

Boltonians are eager to stem this menace, but it has already deteriorated further. Nearby Leigh has recently seen the Boars Head become "Shergars"—perhaps the only pub in the country named after tinned dog food.

Sausage roll

I AM thinking of entering the publishing game with a book of alternative pub names. My favourite so far is the nickname of the long-closed Cock & Pye in Colchester. Locals referred to it as the Prick & Pastry.

Eyeful Tower

I INTEND to give a prize to the most ludicrous pub conversions. The front runners are "Francs" of Openshaw and Stockport's "Far Pavilions".

Francs, formerly the Drovers Inn, will be noticed by travellers on the Ashton Old Road thanks to the discreet addition of a 15-foot scale model of the Eiffel Tower to its roof.

The Far Pavilions, on the other hand, prefers the two-prong attack, first attracting passers-by with an alluring six-foot illuminated pith helmet and then keeping them entranced by piping jungle noises throughout its bars.

By George!

A PRESS release informs us that Chef and Brewer, a Watney-Mann company, is changing the names of four of its subsidiaries "to improve management contact with licensees".

Knowing that you will all wish to note these facts in your social diaries, we publish the press release details as follows:

"The St. George's Taverns name will disappear in the South-east, North-west and South-west, leaving just one company with the St. George's Taverns name in the North-east. Lanchester Taverns (North) is being renamed Tudor Taverns, with Lanchester Taverns (South) retaining its title.

"St. George's Taverns (N-W) becomes Herald Taverns, St. George's Taverns (S-W) is renamed Richmond Taverns and St. George's Taverns (S-E) is now Raven Taverns."

All clear? Good. See you in the Huckleberry on Friday.

Nice bouquet

A MANUAL on how to be a successful pub host includes the following:

"Use a deodorant daily and change socks or stockings every day. Change underclothes frequently and avoid using too much perfume or aftershave."

Missing link

DURING a TV tasting of bottled beers on the BBC's "Food and Drink" programme, presenter Henry Kelly's suggested link line from a film item on Barbara Cartland's romantic meals, to the strong ale session in the studio was: "And now from one Old Peculiar to another . . ."

The producer was not amused and cut the Irishman's wicked wit.

Chilli Con Barmy

ALEXEI Sayle, while in the East Midlands, told Sunday Mirror readers:

"In Nottingham I fancied a hot pie so I went into a pub which said 'Hottye Pies, Cooked and Cured Hammes' and asked for same. They looked at me as if I was barmy and was asking for grilled antelope.

"All they had, like every other pub, was rolls or stale moussaka. When the brewers write olde worlde nonsense outside their pubs they could at least be honest.

"They should write 'Ye Noisiest Videyo Machines in All of Ye Christendome' or 'Fynest Watery Lagers For Ye Yobs In Ye Anoraks' and 'Munificent Microwaved Moussaka and Olde Englyshe Chilli Con Carnye Served By the Formyca Foodye Bar'."

Waste matter

THEY don't mince words Down Under. At the end of a book, the author adds the following conclusion: "If my opinions on the Australian advertising scene have offended anyone inside or outside the industry, I would like you to know deep down from the bottom of my heart that I don't give a shit."

Burnt fingers

DON'T try to find a bed for the night in Saffron Waldon by using the 1984 Automobile Association's Touring Book of Great Britain.

Two of three historic inns listed are unable to offer you hospitality. The Rose & Crown, which the AA insists is worth "special attention" actually burned down 15 years ago. While the other, the Sun Inn, noted a local historian, "has never been open as far back as I can remember. And I was born in 1902."

Knot serious

A SOUTH Devon pub has started a campaign to preserve what its guvnor regards as an important part of Britain's heritage—the dying breed of hankie-on-the-head holidaymakers.

Bomb shock

MUNITIONS researchers in Sydney have reported that (refilled) cans of Fosters lager are a great substitute for smoke grenades (honest). They are already in use in the Australian Army—producing a red, blue, orange and green haze—where authentic smoke-bombs, like authentic beers, are in short supply.

Up the pole

IND COOPE pubs in the Herts/Bucks/Beds trading area have been deluged with leaflets and posters urging drinkers to get on the Benskins Redskins Trail.

The idea of the promotion is for Benskins drinkers to collect a series of "totem pole tokens" and then complete a humorous couplet.

The first two lines, supplied by Ind Coope's heap clever marketing pale faces, begin: "An accomplished brewer named Benskin, Had a beer one night with a Redskin . . ."

One malevolent CAMRA person, who clearly did not enter into the Big White Spirit of the thing, completed his form: "But the brave's tomahawk, Came down with a squawk, And off came the poor brewer's *"&@"?."

Ind Coope probably think that is a bit near the bone. But then what else rhymes with Benskin?

Warm beer

RAY Thuillez is not a rude Breton toast, but the name of an ingenious licensee from Burnham in suburban Slough.

Concerned about the effect of sub-zero temperatures on the flavour of his Courage Directors, he determined to find a means of selling a "warm" pint in spite of the freeze.

When beer was coming from the cellars of the George at 32 deg Fahrenheit, Ray found that cooking a pint for 60 seconds in the pub microwave on a "medium" setting returned the ale to proper drinking temperature of over 50 deg.

Last straw

AN off-licence in Basingstoke has become the victim of a series of bizarre burglaries. The thieves do not break in but instead stick a bent coathanger through the letter box, hook a bottle, unscrew the top, and steal the booze by sucking it through a straw. In three separate incidents the suckers have gone through six litres of wine and vermouth.

Fitter name

JOURNALIST John Clements was dismayed to find that the Danes do not seem to grasp the idea of British pub titles. In a recent article in a Danish magazine his reference to the "Prospect of Whitby" was translated as the "Prospect of Whisky".

BOBBY BEERS

A-HEAD OF THE BEST

POLICE RECORD: Beers from Randall's Brewery on Guernsey are known as Bobby Ales – and used to feature a policeman's helmet as their logo!

Softly, softly

WHEN an application for a dinner-dance extension at the Lively Lady pub in Leicester came before the magistrates, Inspector Peter Allen of the local constabulary objected on the grounds that the police had received complaints from residents about the noise from the pub when previous extensions had been allowed.

And who were responsible for such anti-social behaviour? None other than the local CID, who hold regular dinner-dances in the hostelry. The magistrates granted the application when they heard that the pub had been sound-proofed.

Boys in loo

HAVE you heard the one about the 14 policemen in the ladies lavatory at the Great British Beer Festival? An unlikely story, you may think, but honest, officer, it's true. It happened like this:

On the final Saturday night, it is traditional for staff to dress up a little (or a lot in some cases). Press oficer Jim Webster, who was helping out behind one of the bars, had donned a policeman's helmet, not one of the Toy Town variety but the genuine article kindly donated by one of the site officers.

Giving a passable impression of PC 49 from the neck upwards, luckless Jim was bending over one of the casks filling a glass, when he received a heavy tap on the shoulder.

"I turned round and the hall went dark." There, looming above him, was a very large Chief Inspector. "Where did you get that hat?" boomed the mountain of authority, or words to that effect.

Jim, his knees knocking together in time with the steel band, garbled an explanation. Far from satisfied, the stern lawman announced he was going to the organiser's office.

Jim hurried ahead, fearing a life sentence or worse

for impersonating a police officer's head. But in the Press room, adjoining the organiser's office, an even more worrying sight met his wildly staring eyes.

Happily entrenched in the room were 14 more uniformed coppers, carefully investigating the contents of a cask of Timothy Taylor's Landlord, the Beer of the Year, in the course of their duty. When Jim told them their boss was on the way, panic set in.

They demanded to know where the back door was. There wasn't one. So, they tumbled into the ladies loo. The gents was too risky; the Inspector might have felt a call of nature.

Fortunately, it proved a convenient—if cramped—hiding place, until the coast was clear. And then they slipped out, two by two, into the happy crowd.

Evening all.

Court out

WHEN F. E. Smith, later Lord Birkenhead, was still a practising barrister, he described his client, to the court, as having been "drunk as a judge".

Judge: **"The expression, Mr. Smith, is 'drunk as a Lord.'"**

Smith: **"As you please, my Lord."**

Sexy beer

A BREWERY in Schiltigheim, France, is conducting experiments on its workforce. Ten workers have been asked to drink quantities of a new lager which has been laced with herbal extract designed to improve the sex drive.

One of the guinea pigs told French newsmen: "After six glasses of this stuff I'm raring to go. Normally after a night on la biere a man is good for nothing."

Silk Solution

NAUGHTY but nice department: A sign with shapely legs, suspenders and black stockings, which upset women lawyers in Bristol, has coaxed a smile and a happy gurgle from local babies.

Halls gave the offending sign from their Silks cocktail bar to CAMRA's Avon branch, who auctioned it at the Great Western Beer Festival. It raised £65 out of a total of £283 for the special baby care unit at Southmead Hospital.

Which just goes to prove that even black stockings have a silver lining.

NAUGHTY but nasty department: Meanwhile, Ind Coope have put away the canes and gymslips, and dropped their experiment with "schoolgirl barmaids" in a St. Trinians style pub in Derby, called "Trinians".

"The schoolgirl theme did not work as successfully as we had hoped, and the pub now needs a new image," explained the Burton headmaster. How about a kinky leather pub called Whips next?

Chief whip

A CAMRA delegation to the EEC Commission in Brussels, to discuss such worthy matters as relaxing the brewers' grip on the tied trade, were confronted by one Eurocrat with the splendid title of Director for Abuse of Dominant Positions.

Bad vibrations

GLASGOW landlord Robert Salmon of the small but perfectly formed Granny Black's Bar was upset when the bench chopped his licence:

"I'm shattered. It means the city licensing board believes the stories of girls with vibrators and bananas running around the pub touching up customers." One was a plain-clothes police officer.

Round in circles

IT'S time, gentlemen, please, someone talked a bit of sense into the Independent Broadcasting Authority. Or at least kept the bottle farther away from the table the next time they discuss drinks advertising controls.

Their latest rules for radio and television contain such gems as banning any references to "buying a round". Explained a spokesman: "The idea of an obligation to buy one's round is sometimes felt to encourage excessive drinking. This will, of course, not normally prevent a scene showing someone merely buying a drink for their friends."

Sadly, no one has yet worked out the difference between buying a round and buying drinks for the lads.

I kid you not

SPOTTED in an Eldridge Pope pub in deepest Dorset, on the door to the gentlemen's toilet: "Faust. You're getting closer to finding a truly great lager."

THE SELLAFIELD ARMS
BARS
"I'M SORRY, SIR, BUT WE ONLY SELL BRIGHT BEER"

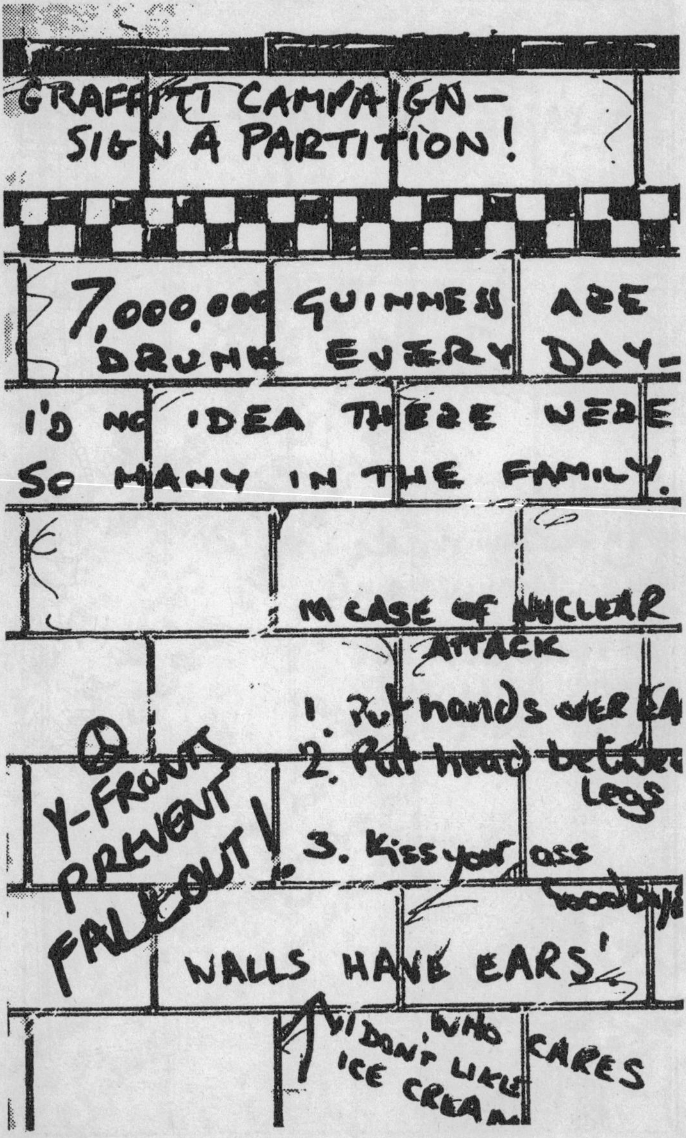
GRAFFITI CAMPAIGN—
SIGN A PARTITION!
7,000,000 GUINNESS ARE DRUNK EVERY DAY.
I'D NO IDEA THERE WERE SO MANY IN THE FAMILY.
IN CASE OF NUCLEAR ATTACK
1. Put hands over
2. Put head between legs
3. Kiss your ass
Y-FRONTS PREVENT FALLOUT!
WALLS HAVE EARS
I DON'T LIKE ICE CREAM
WHO CARES

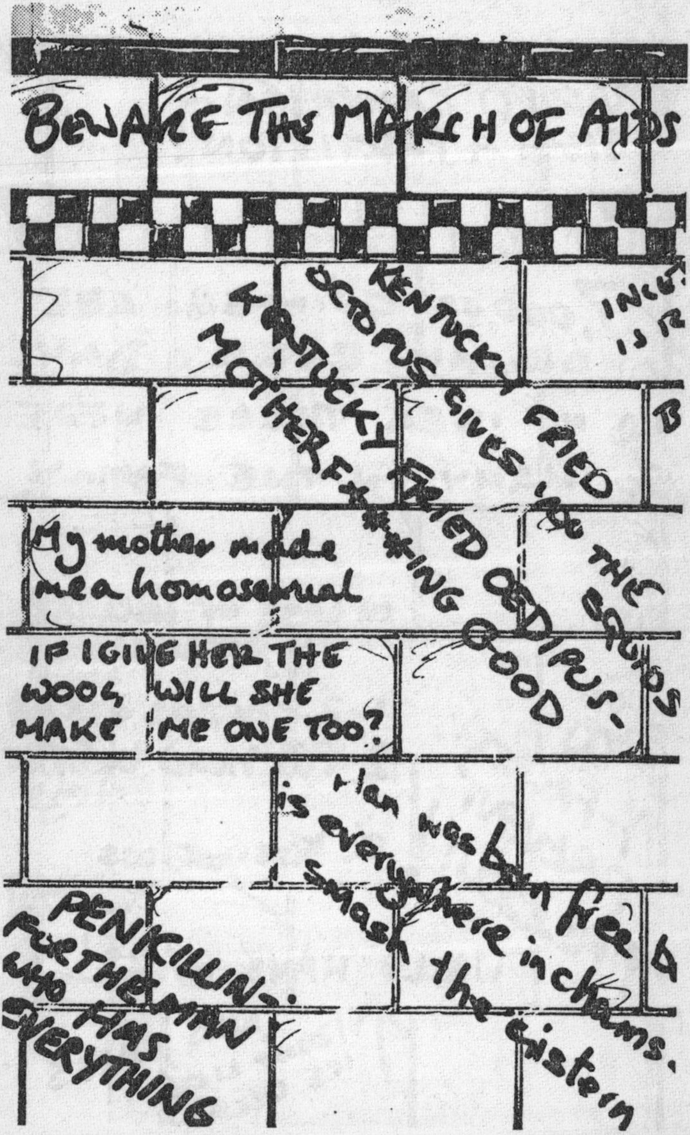
BEWARE THE MARCH OF AIDS
KENTUCKY FRIED OCTOPUS GIVES YOU THE SQUIDS
KENTUCKY FRIED OEDIPUS-
MOTHERF**KING GOOD
My mother made me a homosexual
IF I GIVE HER THE WOOL, WILL SHE MAKE ME ONE TOO?
Man was born free
is everywhere in chains.
Smash the cistern
PENKILLIN -
FOR THE MAN WHO HAS EVERYTHING

Brandex
SENSATIONS
BUY 144 + COMMIT A GROSS INDECENCY !!
BUY ME AND STOP ONE - BUY 2 AND BE ONE JUMP AHEAD!
50P PACK OF THREE
This machine's empty - again!
YOUR FOOT!
UNK.

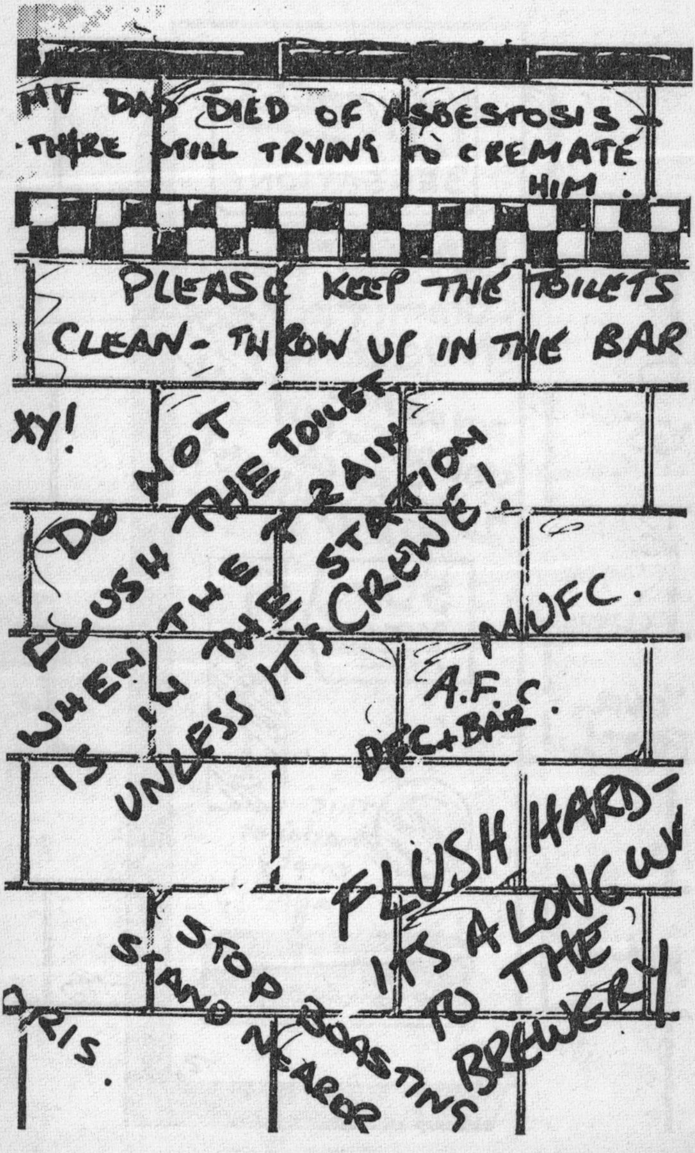
MY DAD DIED OF ASBESTOSIS - THERE STILL TRYING TO CREMATE HIM.
PLEASE KEEP THE TOILETS CLEAN - THROW UP IN THE BAR
XY!
DO NOT FLUSH THE TOILET WHEN THE TRAIN IS IN THE STATION UNLESS IT'S CREWE!
MUFC.
A.F.C.
FLUSH HARD - ITS A LONG W
TO THE BREWERY
STOP
BOASTING
RIS.

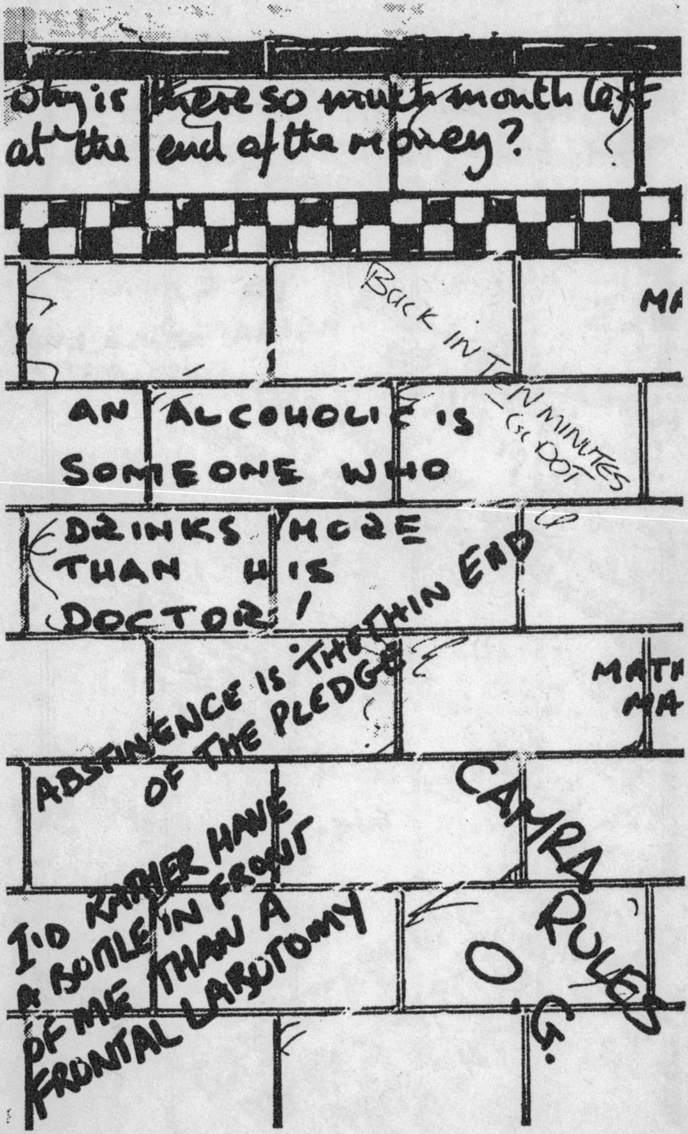
Why is there so much month left at the end of the money?
BACK IN TEN MINUTES
GODOT
AN ALCOHOLIC IS SOMEONE WHO DRINKS MORE THAN HIS DOCTOR!
ABSTINENCE IS THE THIN END OF THE PLEDGE
CAMRA RULES O.G.
I'D RATHER HAVE A BOTTLE IN FRONT OF ME THAN A FRONTAL LABOTOMY

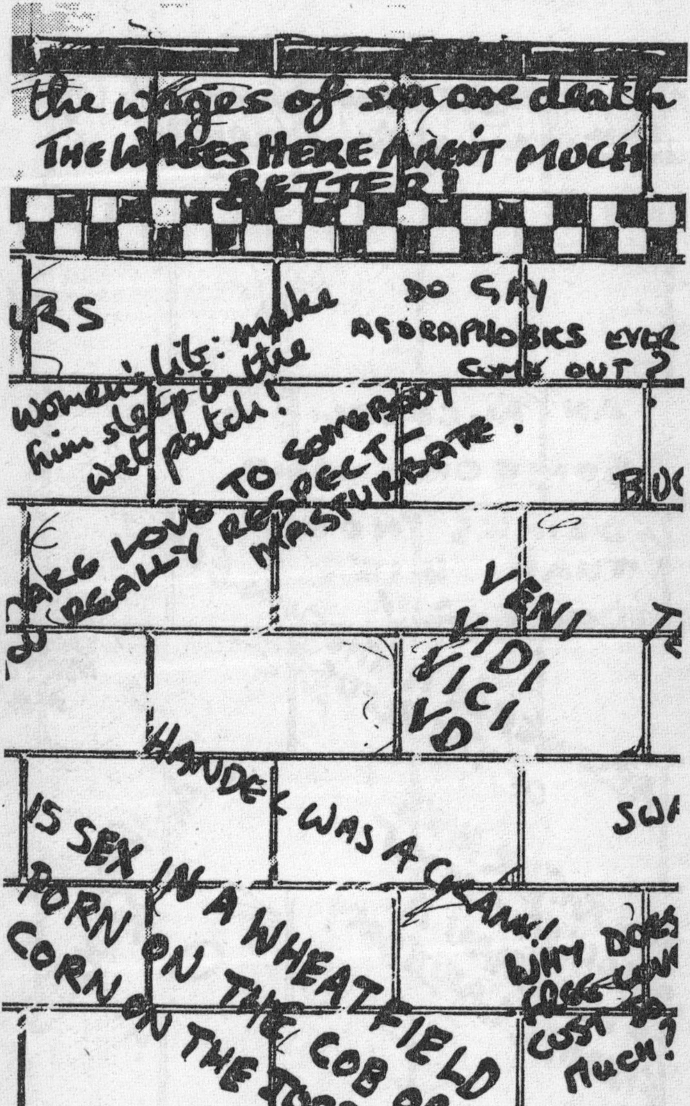
the wages of sin are death
THE WAGES HERE AREN'T MUCH BETTER!
DO GAY AGORAPHOBICS EVER COME OUT?
women's lib: make him sleep in the wet patch!
MAKE LOVE TO SOMEBODY YOU REALLY RESPECT — MASTURBATE.
VENI VIDI VICI VD
HANDEL WAS A CRANK!
IS SEX IN A WHEATFIELD PORN ON THE COB OR CORN ON THE JOB?

Aid memoir

ONE of the houses in Neil Hanson's "100 Classic Country Pubs" book might have been included for its notice board alone. The Castle Inn at Lydford at the time of inspection was doing its bit for health education by advertising a lecture on AIDS to the local community association.

The speaker? Rear Admiral Cox.

Old Croaker

EVERYONE knows there are hops in beer. But the Three Horseshoes in Oulton, West Yorkshire, also has some hops in its pub cellar—in the shape of Fred the Toad. Licensee John Fletcher says that Fred is now so tame, he will come to heel when his name is called.

Pub sunk

A LANDLORD had to cry "abandon pub" when The Barge Inn, a converted drain barge, started to sink to the bottom of the River Ouse in York.

As the Theakston's Bitter poured, the river flooded in through a sudden hole. Fortunately, none of the crew of customers was hurt as they barged out to safety. Women and pints first, of course.

No shorts

WHERE do they pick 'em from? Grand Metropolitan's CC soft drinks company is about to launch an American carbonated citrus drink in Britain. Its name is Squirt.

Ordering a bottle should be guaranteed to get you thrown out of most bars. Barman: "What was that? A pint of bitter and a . . .?" Customer: "Little Squirt."

Tight fit

IF you broke one of your toes when you tried on a new pair of shoes over Christmas, it's probably because Magnus of Northampton, the outsize footwear specialists, have been sending out their boots during December with a nip of Mackinlay's Scotch whisky inside.

Palace problem

HIGH spot of the opening of the Great British Beer Festival at Alexandra Palace in North London was the sight of some splendid, traditional horse-drawn drays pulling their wares up the hill to the palace.

There were a few snags. Some of the drivers from out of town weren't too used to the Great Wen and asked directions for "the palace". One was sent to Crystal Palace in the far reaches of South London.

Another found himself at Buckingham Palace. We have it on good authority that, when asked where she wanted the beer delivered, the lady of the house was not amused.

Too sharp

REPORTING the splendid news of a small brewery on the Isle of Lewis at the Borve House Hotel, the Scottish Sunday Standard records that the hotel-cum-brewery has a chequered past:

"Borve House won fleeting notoriety a few years back when it was raided by a large contingent of the local constabulary anxious to find if its table licence was being abused.

"At the subsequent trial, a procession of crofters trooped into the witness box to testify that their primary purpose in going to the hotel on the night in question had been 'to get a sandwich'.

"An exasperated procurator fiscal eventually put it to one old gentleman, that if it was a sandwich he wanted he would be quicker having it at home.

"*'We don't have the sliced bread in these parts,' was the reply.*

"*'Wouldn't you be quicker cutting it?' pressed the fiscal.*

"*'That,' said the crofter, 'would depend on the knife.'*

'At the end of a very long day, the sheriff returned the classic Scottish verdict of Not Proven. Honours were even."

Hopless

WHAT is the difference between a dead frog and a pint of Ben Truman? Answer: There are more hops in a dead frog . . .

Blasted bog

AN explosive lavatory at the Old Crown Inn, Twerton, near Bath, has been causing great consternation. The flash in the pan in the gents blasted the WC off the floor and into pieces.

Council engineers have yet to identify the cause, but a likely explanation is that the chain reaction was caused by a build-up of gas in the drains below the bowl. I wonder what the locals were drinking?

Meanwhile, a replacement bowl has been installed, but customers are a little wary of sitting on the job any length of time.

The ability of Burton-brewed beers to energise the lower intestines are legendary, but aren't Marstons going just a bit far with this mat?

Rising Runs

BASS must be back to its best. The Rising Sun in Stevenage is advertising "traditional rear ales".

Open all hours

ST. ALBANS' historic city centre boasts, among its delights, the splendidly beamed old Peahen Hotel, a McMullen's emporium with a strict dividing line twixt respectable lounge and boisterous bar.

Short of staff, the landlord took on a new bar manager one day and, against his usual practice of breaking them in gently in the lounge, plunged the callow youth into the fray of the public, with a few words of advice about prices and how to work the optic.

It was a Wednesday. Come 2.20 p.m. and the youth rang the bell, calling out proudly to the throng: "Last orders, please." One chancer, just blowing the froth off his pint of Country, inquired: "What did you say?"

The lad gulped nervously and repeated: "Last orders, if it pleases you."

"No, it doesn't bleedin' please me," the toper replied belligerently. "Where have you been all my life? It's market day in St. Albans. The pubs don't shut, right?"

"Sorry, sir," the lad said obsequiously. "It's my first day. What would you like?"

An hour-and-a-half later, he approached the landlord, who was cashing up in the ominously empty lounge.

"Excuse me, sir," said the lad, "but when do I get relieved?"

The landlord looked him up and down in sheer disbelief. "What the hell are you doing here at 4 o'clock in the afternoon?"

"But it's market day," the lad replied. "I'm still serving."

The landlord turned a nasty shade of ashen, expecting the Old William to burst into his bar at any moment. "But there's no extension on market day in St. Albans," he croaked, then rushed to the public, where eight cheerful and distinctly legless boozers were still going strong.

No bar

JOURNALIST Ray Bryant, of the Reading Evening Post, has been banging the drum for more flexible pub opening hours.

Looking back nostalgically at a holiday spent in Eire, he related that after arriving too early at a pub in County Cork, he was told:

"I'm sorry, sir, we don't open till four—but will you be having one while you're waiting."

Election special

ROBIN Quinn's Dragon Cider Company optimistically produced a real Somerset cider called "Thatcher's Ruin". Alas, the company has failed. The winding up meeting was held in Cardiff on June 11, 1987.

Bubbling along

WATNEY'S Wales and West division has solved the problem of falling sales of keg beer. The Western Daily Press reports that Watneys are converting 80 of their company cars to run on gas instead of petrol.

Pillow talk

CAMRA stalwart Peter Lerner is having some difficulty spreading the Pub Preservation Group gospel. His latest feature for one of Hertfordshire's up-market magazines for county folk was attacked by gremlins at the printers. "Two local pubs in our county town of Hertford," waxed the lyrical Peter, "are to be knocked through to be turned into one-bedroomed bars."

Chile reception

A VERY bad taste award goes to the manager of Oddbins off-licence in Covent Garden for his promotion of Chilean Wines.

"Don't torture yourself wondering whether this wine is good," began the notice, ". . . it's not a bad price considering how much their electricity bills are."

Visitors to London's most popular tourist area could also savour his description of *Concha y Toro:* "A Chilean ball game wherein the balls are repeatedly bounced against a wall with a bat until they burst or the prisoner confesses."

Bass monkeys

THE weather wasn't too bright at the opening of the Canalside Inn, built for Stoke-on-Trent's National Garden Festival. As Lord Mayor John Burkin and guests set about toasting the new pub with Draught Bass, they noticed that the British winter had frozen over the beer in their glasses.

"I'd never had Bass on the rocks," quipped the Mayor.

Stretching it

THE new landlord at Fosters, Upper Brook St., Manchester, is reported to be Mr. Thomas Michael William Patrick Spiral Staircase Katanga Katanga Redstep O'Dowd. Honest.

"The beer's good here but there's too much going on!"

KEITH WATERHOUSE

"God, here's another one—where the hell are they all coming from?"

Stepping on the Moon

GEORGE ORWELL'S favourite boozer was "The Moon under Water". It was a comfortable, ugly place, with ornamental mirrors behind the bar, cast-iron fireplaces, a florid ceiling stained dark yellow by tobacco-smoke, a stuffed bull's head over the mantelpiece—but without sham roof-beams, ingle-nooks or barmaids who called you "Ducky".

Upstairs you could get a cut off the joint, two veg and boiled jam roll; downstairs you could get liver-sausage sandwiches, mussels, cheese and pickles. The pride and joy of the pub was its garden where you could drink draught cider while the children played. But there was no piano or radio on the premises, and darts-playing was confined to the public bar. The only possible snag about "The Moon under Water", as described by Orwell in 1946, was that it did not exist. It was his idea of the perfect pub, and he had yet to find it.

Actually, Orwell was wrong—both in the sense of being mistaken and of being inaccurate. His ideal pub did exist but it wasn't called "The Moon under Water"—it went under a variety of aliases, most of them affectionate nicknames such as "The Mucky Duck". Sometimes it had a garden though usually it didn't, but rustic benches under old oak trees apart, it had most of the qualities that not only Orwell, but even those fat Georgian essayists who drivelled on about Your English Ale at Your English Inn, would have required. It was thriving well into the late nineteen-sixties, and I will tell you what's happened to it since.

"The Moon" was originally owned by Buggins's Brewery, a family concern so tiny that its entire output could be distributed throughout London by three teams of

drayhorses. Buggins sold out to Duggins's Draught, Duggins in turn merged with Coggins's Keg, and finally the whole mini-conglomerate was taken over by Consolidated Piss.

Just because Consolidated Piss are as interested in commercial property, bingo halls, hamburger-dromes and roofing felt as they are in beer, it has been suggested that "The Moon's" decline dates from when it ceased to function as an independent corner pub and became one of a chain of 15,000 "outlets". This is hardly fair. Its fortunes were on the turn as long ago as 1951, when Len, Mine Host as was under the old Buggins's patronage, had a bit of a brainstorm. Though Len is now remembered with affection there is no doubt that he was one of the most stupid men ever to be given free rein over a public house. In the euphoria of the Festival of Britain, Len was visited by the delusion that it was time "The Moon" had a face-lift. "What the class of people we get in here wants," he

persuaded the directors of Buggins's Brewery, "is more your modern."

So down came the ornamental mirrors and the stuffed bull's head over the mantelpiece. The cast-iron fireplaces went to the scrapyard. New plastic tables, which could be wiped over with a cloth for all the world as if they were topped with marble like the ones that had graced the saloon bar for nigh on a century, were installed. And very pretty they were, if a bit rocky—much prettier, and not much rockier, than the ones that have since replaced them fifteen times over. They were milk-chocolate in colour, cleverly grained to simulate wood, and this theme was reflected in the new false ceiling of imitation walnut tiles —literally reflected, for every second tile lit up at the touch of a switch.

For the wallpaper, Len favoured a theme of scattered cocktail glasses, top hats, and cigarettes in long holders. His new carpet was a random pattern consistent with a navvy having emptied a family pack of potato crisps on the floor and trampled on them. Where the ornamental mirrors had been, he installed illuminated panels—one of them with a rippling neon effect, like a glass-fronted toilet cistern—advertising small bottled drinks.

Well satisfied with his efforts, Len was making a note to do something about the gents' lavvy one of these days when he was summarily thrown out into the street, and a tenant of Duggins's Draught, one Ken, took over.

All we need to know about Ken is that he wore a blazer, addressed his customers as "Squire" or by their initials (Morning, Mr. W., and how's Mr. W. this morning?") and that he introduced to the premises some black plastic ashtrays in the shape of the human hand, an ice-bucket (containing an inch of tepid water) fashioned after a pineapple, and his coup de grace—the cigarette machine. From Ken's regime onwards, "The Moon's" customers were no longer put to the bother of having to jostle at the bar for a packet of fags. They merely had to jostle at the bar for change to put in the cigarette machine.

Ken's crowning ambition—to get rid of the public bar trade and start a Sunday-morning darts league among the cravat-wearers and ladies in trouser-suits—was only half-realised. His successor, Ben, manager for Coggins's Keg, did in fact get rid of the public bar trade (by pulling down a partition and charging saloon bar prices for all drinks served), but he also got rid of the darts-board on the grounds that it took up space. In its place were put a juke

TWO PLOUGHMANS... D'YOU WANT ANY MANURE?
PUB GRUB

box, a fruit machine, a television set, a pool-table, and later an ingenious electronic tennis game costing 50p a go. The infra-red oven, which could heat up a Cellophane-wrapped cheese-and-chutney toasted sandwich in three seconds, was another of Ben's innovations.

The situation a year or two after "The Moon's" mahogany exterior had been painted buttercup yellow to welcome it into the bosom of the Consolidated Piss family of hostelries, was as follows.

Ben, the manager, had built up a good trade among young executives from the office blocks that had recently sprung up around "The Moon". They liked the toasted sandwiches and they were fascinated by the electronic tennis machine. The new decor—pegboard ceiling and imitation plywood panelling—did not offend them. The barmen wore proper barmen's jackets and spoke respectfully. The gents' boasted a paper-towel machine, which occasionally contained paper towels.

For those who found the beer unspeakable, there was a drinkable Spanish Chablis at £1·20 a small glass. But most did not find the beer unspeakable. None of them, of course, remembered the original Buggins's or Duggins's barrelled beers: they had been brought up on Coggins's Keg, which they called "draught". When Coggins's keg was taken off the market and a massive TV campaign ("I couldn't 'alf do with a Piss") pushed the virtues of Consolidated Piss Original Drayhouse Ale, they were persuaded that they had switched to a stronger and more manly brew.

"It's claimed to be the last men-only bar in the country"

Within its new limitations, then, "The Moon" was still a successful pub when Consolidated Piss sold out to their own property division, who promptly pulled it down. However, the licence remains and there is every hope that there will be a new pub—"The New Moon"—in the basement of the showroom-and-office complex now being built on the site.

What form it will take, Consolidated Piss are not sure. They are anxious to move with the times, but they have had their fingers burnt lately. A few years ago they began to jolly up some of their pubs by turning them into replicas of paddle-steamers, barns, tram-sheds and so forth; but the novelty quickly wore off and they lost money. Nowadays there seems to be a demand for traditional pubs, to compete with the craze for Edwardian wine bars. Their clever young designer knows where he can get his hands on some ornamental mirrors, marble tables, cast-iron fireplaces and various knick-knacks such as a stuffed bull's head. He can also get hold of some original Victorian ceiling-moulds and there is a chemical process by which a ceiling can be stained dark yellow as if by tobacco-smoke. But, of course, all this stuff comes expensive, and it must inevitably be reflected in the price of the beer.

Keith Waterhouse

Tap-room tale

THE day the great Yorkshire brewer Joshua Tetley died, Sam Smith contacted John Smith to say: "We might be competitors, but let's settle our differences for one day and, as a mark of respect, go to ol' Josh's funeral together." John agreed.

As they arrived in Leeds early, Sam suggested to John that they went for a jar. Once again, John agreed, and off they went into a nearby free house.

Sam said: "Since it's a day for letting bygones be bygones, I'll have a pint of John Smith's."

Supping their pints, John said: "Here we are, two great brewing rivals; you pick me up to go to Joshua Tetley's funeral and now, Sam, you're drinking John Smith's bitter. What's brought this on?"

Sam replied: "Well, John, we don't want to go to church reeking of beer, do we?"

Grassed

THREE people who were arrested in a park in Rushden, Northants, surrounded by beer cans and a partly-drunk bottle of rum, denied that they were drunk when they appeared in court.

When one of the trio was asked by the prosecution to explain why he claimed not to be drunk after admitting he had consumed four pints of beer as well as some rum, he replied: "Because the beer was Watney's."

Strong drain

ONE of the most potent beers in Britain can only be found in the sewers of Sheffield.

It's all to do with a certain alcohol-free lager called Barbican, brewed by Bass in Sheffield.

Barbican starts out as Carling Black Label but, after fermentation, the alcohol is removed by a "top secret" method—believed to be distillation—that renders the stuff gutless.

The offending alcohol is then poured away down a drain which is kept locked and barred at all times.

This is to keep off the hordes of drinkers who have just tasted Barbican for the first time and then rush to the brewery to demand their alcohol back.

I'm worried about Pendleton, he went in there yesterday!

Unfit fluid

WHEN workers at the Whitbread Salford brewery produced a list of demands to settle their industrial dispute, high on the list was a complaint that their beer allowance was undrinkable.

Mad crowd

THERE'S nothing new about bad beer. In Tess of the d'Urbervilles, published in 1891, Thomas Hardy, who knew a good drop when he tasted one, made this acid comment on some of the beer practices of the time:

"The chief pleasure of these philosophers lay in going every Saturday night, when work was done, to Chaseborough [Cranborne, Dorset], a decayed market-town, two or three miles distant; and, returning in the small hours of the next morning, to spend Sunday in sleeping off the dyspeptic effects of the curious compounds sold to them as beer by the monopolisers of the once independent inns."

Watney mystery

THE London Evening Standard reported that a drayman and a driver employed by Watney in Whitechapel had each been jailed for four months after being convicted of selling beer they had stolen from their tanker and replaced with water. How on earth were they found out?

Worm solution

THERE once was a famous temperance lecturer, the high point of whose address against the demon drink was to produce at the right moment a glass which she filled with water and then another glass which she filled with gin.

From a pocket came a matchbox containing two worms. With a theatrical flourish one worm was dropped in the water and the other in the gin. Both worms wriggled for a while and, predictably enough, the one in the gin expired rather more quickly than the one in the water. Just as it did so she pointed to the sky and asked, with a dramatic gesture: "What does this prove?"

At that point someone at the back said: "If you have worms, drink gin."

Dead Admiral

FOLLOWING complaints that the butterflies at his Butterfly Safari in Friarbourne were so intoxicated on fermented nectar that they were flying into visitors, Mr. John Ellerton said: "If your life was only three weeks long, you would probably be a heavy drinker too."

Ever noticed how reluctant people are to admit that they're drunk? The euphemisms for being squiffy (see what I mean) are endless . . . and are not confined to these isles. According to the New York Sunday Times, a number of modern terms have been introduced to complement the best known STIFF. In the age of the automobile, drunks are now referred to as being WRECKED or TOTALLED (i.e. a total right-off). Other expressions for the sublime state include HAMMERED, BULLETPROOFED, BUZZED, LAID OUT, POLLUTED, OFF NICELY, FACED, GIFFED and STRETCHED. Neatest by far is WATCHING THE ANTS RACE.

SPORTS

Out again

IT seems it is not only within the hallowed confines of Yorkshire cricket that Geoffrey Boycott causes controversy. Miles away in Bedford his dismissal has also sparked a row.

Landlord Mike Dewer of the Cricketers Arms spent £170 on a new sign for his pub depicting Sir Geoffrey. But brewers Greene King raised their finger and sent the painted man back to the pavilion, insisting on their first choice, W. G. Grace.

They fear the sight of the awkward batsman may put people off their drink.

Middle stump

A cautionary tale of the perils of supping ale from Christopher Martin-Jenkins' *The Book of Cricket Eccentrics.*

It concerns one Bobby Peel, a Yorkshire and England professional in the late 19th century who, towards the end of an illustrious cricketing career, invested in the tenancy of a public house. Alas, his two careers did not mix well.

On several occasions Peel, much the worse for beer, had to be ordered or else carried off the field of play. Most notably on the occasion when he started bowling at the sight-screen, having failed to notice that the batsman was in fact standing 22 yards in the opposite direction.

But his coup de grace came in the wake of his finest achievement with the bat. Having written himself indelibly into the pages of Wisden by contributing 210 not out to the eighth wicket partnership of 262 with his captain, Lord Hawke (an English record to this day), Peel embarked on a major celebration.

Still toxic the following morning, he walked onto the Edgbaston turf and promptly relieved himself in the outfield. It was too much for his Lordship who forbade him ever to play in his side again.

He seems to get rather careless after opening time.

Ferret tale

WHITBREAD have been reviewing their sponsorship deals for sporting events. The County Championship next year perhaps? No, they have gone into ferret-racing.

At the Black Dog in Yapton (geddit!), the Whitbread Golden Cup was contested on September 15. The Heineken Trophy and Samuel Whitbread Stakes were also run but, surprise, surprise, no Mackeson Stoat Handicap.

Man's best fiend

THE minutes of CAMRA's East Midlands regional meeting, held at the Swan-in-the-Rushes, Loughborough, read: "The meeting adjourned for ten minutes . . . after the landlord's dog had been sick over the Regional Organiser."

Skittled out

NOW that concerted action from the Football Association is clearing the terraces of yobs and rowdies, maybe the Sports Minister should turn his attention to the West Somerset Skittles League.

After one match at the Arew Arms in Crowcombe, licensee Norma Bremner remarked that "It took us three hours to clear up the terrible mess". Apparently the visiting team went on the rampage after players' drinks had been repeatedly spiked with vodka.

As a lesson to us all, skittles officials have banned the team forever from playing in the league and banned each player from competition for five years.

Out of shape

HEART-WARMING, isn't it, the way the big brewers are so in touch with their customers at the grass-roots, sensitive to every nuance of regional taste and culture.

Take Tetleys, the Northern arm of mighty Allied. They opened a new pub in St. Helens, Lancs, called the Footballer.

It's slap next to the football ground, so the name is apt. Trouble was, the inn sign had a *round* ball.

A few local trouble-makers and malcontents pointed out to Tetleys that St. Helens is a bastion of Rugby League and round balls aren't too popular in the vicinity of the stadium.

Tetley's rushed an artist to the pub who, somewhat red-faced, nipped up a step-ladder and deftly transformed the ball into the spheroid shape.

Early bath, Allied!

Good player

QUOTE of the year for 1986 came from Scottish & Newcastle's marketing manager, Ron Woodman, commenting on the brewery's interest in a deal to bring over World Cup soccer star, Maradona, on the lines of the arrangement that took Kevin Keegan to Newcastle.

"We got tremendous value for Keegan. He made personal appearances, meeting thousands and thousands of our customers, without ever once presenting the wrong image by being seen with a glass of beer in his hand."

Arrers wear

FIRST they ruined the ale, then they plasticated the pub. Now they want to commercialise the last bastion of traditional pub life: darts.

Yes, folks, its commercialisation time for the old bristle board and "arrers". Admiral Sports of Leicester, who brought a touch of the nasties to English football when they got the copyright for the team strip, have bought up the British Darts Organisation.

Admiral will market exclusive gear for playing darts: scarlet trousers and an assortment of shirts, special—I kid you not—darts shoes and, as if you hadn't guessed, Admiral hold-alls for carrying the stuff around.

The gear is designed, say Admiral, to be "socially acceptable" so that darts players can spend an evening in the pub without appearing conspicuous. Of course, everyone in my local wears scarlet trousers and carries his small change in an Admiral hold-all.

Third glass

"WE recognise the importance of women in pubs," said Vaux Brewery managing director, Richard Petit, on launching a new third-pint beer glass "for ladies". If the Sunderland lads recognise women's importance—why don't they give them a decent size drink?

Got time for a quick one?

No Brains

THE proliferation of new beer brands from small brewers can create problems. The landlord of Tylers, Llangynwyd, near Bridgend in Mid-Glamorgan, was perplexed and puzzled when 30 regulars trooped in one evening and demanded pints of "Fairclough".

Wales is awash in new brews but the landlord had never heard of this one. The drinkers were adamant that the pub was selling such a beverage and dragged the protesting publican outside.

There, alongside the brewer's name, was another sign announcing, proudly, "Fairclough". The pub was being refurbished and the name of the building firm was (all together now) . . .

Dem dry bones

"DOMINOES is about as mild and sinless a game as any in the world."

I have always admired mark Twain, but when he said that, he was talking through his hat. I wish he could have been at my local on a match night.

Along with a number of the essentials of modern civilisation—such as gunpowder and folding money—dominoes originated in ancient China. The story goes that they were designed to represent all the possible throws with two dice. Apparantly Chinese dominoes have no blanks.

Dominoes were in use in France and Italy in the eighteenth century and were brought to England in the late 1700s by French prisoners of war. What is not known is how they got from China to Europe. It is stretching things a bit to imagine Marco Polo taking on Kublai Khan for two ducats a knock.

The rules of dominoes vary from area to area, and in some places even from pub to pub. There are two basic forms of the game, though. In 'straight' dominoes, each player tries to get rid of all his pieces before the other players. In 'fives and threes' you try to make the spots on the two end pieces add up to a multiple of three or five and the score is usually kept on a crib board.

In the part of England that I come from—the North-West—a set of dominoes goes up to double nine, 55 pieces in all. Until my student days in London I was unaware that there was such a thing as a double-six set. When someone suggested a game of dominoes one night, I was amazed to see the puny little box with its mere sprinkling of bones. And, of course, no-one believed me when I told them about the sets back home. To the Londoner, a double nine sounds as outlandish as the seventeen of spades.

Next term I returned armed with a double nine, which I carried around in my pocket everywhere I went. I won more money from people who were willing to bet that it didn't exist than I ever won from actually playing the game.

Some authorities on dominoes make vague references to sets on which the spots go beyond double nine—even up to double twelve, according to the *Encyclopaedia Britannica.* Really, I can't believe this, although I am willing to concede that it sometimes seems that way. Especially after a full evening's play—or a full evening's drinking, come to that.

Dominoes are often linked with darts. There are darts and dominoes leagues, and darts and dominoes matches are played between the same two pubs at the same venue on the same night. Don't be misled by this, though. I'm told that at the best public schools you either play cricket or you row—never both. Well, it's much the same in the best public houses—you either dart or domino, and the two groups usually hold each other in mutual contempt.

In our local league the game is 'straight' dominoes—one pair of players against another pair It is a game of deadly seriousness and, I am assured, great skill. To the uninitiated, the meanings of different leads and lines of play appear as complex as the signals which pass between partners in contract bridge. To the initiated they are even more complex!

To keep up this standard, a player needs nerves of steel. I myself retired from competitive play at the age of 33, before I cracked under the tremendous psychological strain.

First, of course, is the pressure from your opponents, who will mercilessly pounce on the slightest mistake. This is only to be expected.

Then there is the referee. Each game is presided over by a hawk-eyed individual ready to punish the tiniest offence against the rules. You may not speak. If you are unable to play, you knock on the table in the time-honoured way. The heinous crime of knocking when you could have played is punished by immediate loss of the game and probably a three-match suspension.

Next, there is your captain—quite often a non-playing one—peering over your shoulder and greeting your every move with an expression of utter disbelief. To him, every game you win is a matter of incredible good luck.

Last, and definitely worst, is the pressure from your own partner. He will undoubtedly criticise every domino you play, blame you for every defeat and take all the credit whenever you win.

After the phenomenal success of darts as a television spectacular, the powers that be must have considered the introduction of dominoes on TV. Rumour has it that it was rejected on the grounds that the commentary would be too boring: "He's played the 8-6. Now double 8. Followed by the 6-3". If this is true, a golden opportunity was missed.

What is needed is the approach of the chess series, 'The Master Game'. Imagine a tense moment on BBC 2's Double

Nine Chips (signature tune: 'Dem bones, dem bones, dem dry bones').

The screen is split three ways. The first picture is a diagram showing the state of play on the table. The second shows a hand of dominoes, and the third, the contorted face of the man about to play.

"I've got to decide whether to play 8-blank or 6-3. Now, let's see. Tony went down with 8-6, the Ramsbottom Gambit. (Domino flashes on diagram.) That means he's got plenty of eights and sixes. Unless of course it's a bluff and he hasn't got any of either.

"Then Spassky followed with the Westhoughton Defence. (Double 8 flashes on diagram.) So he's either short of sixes or he's just getting rid of an awkward double. No, that's not really his style and anyway I want to make the most of my blanks.

"But I must bear in mind that the one on the table with the little chip missing from the corner is the double 6. Yes, I think I'll play the 6-3." This could go on all night, to an audience of millions.

Meanwhile, back in the pub, a warm fire blazes up on a cold winter's evening. Pints rest on the special ledge under the table and the bones rattle out onto its smooth top.

Played for small stakes among old friends, dominoes almost ceases to be a game and becomes a time-hallowed ritual; an affirmation that everything in the universe is in place. The same dominoes are played; the same comments passed. When one old stager plays the double blank he will invariably remark: "Never played for a count-up in me life." Another, every time the double six is played, sighs and murmurs: "Janie Makin"—apparently a reference to some long-legged beauty from his lost youth.

Mark Twain, wherever you are, I apologise. You knew what you were talking about all the time.

Bill Lythgoe

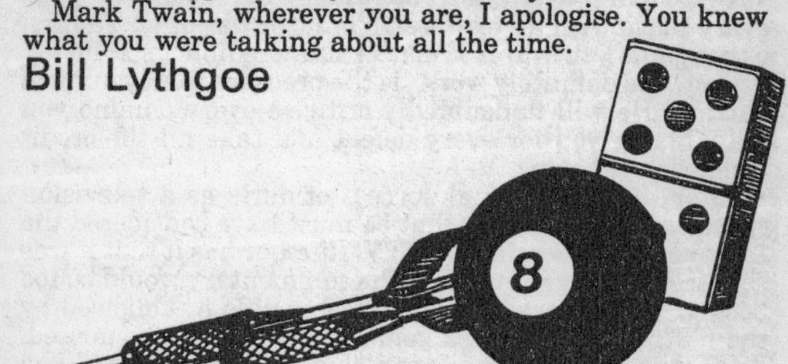

Boozer's guide to going home

MEMORISE these tight tips now. You'll never be able to read them when you've had too many. We cannot guarantee that they will get you home, but at least they may show you where you are going wrong . . .

Symptom

The night is cold and wet, the road is muddy under-foot, and you keep tripping over old bicycle frames.

Possible cause

You were walking in the canal.

Symptom

Lashing rain is coming at you horizontally. Suddenly everything goes white.

Possible cause

You are in a car-wash.

Symptom

The cigarette you have just bought from a slot machine tasted foul and lasted only 10 seconds.

Possible cause

You have just smoked a railway platform ticket.

Symptom

It's taking you far longer than normal to get to the top of the steps. After 15 minutes hard climbing you decide you really must go on that diet.

Possible cause

You are walking up a down escalator.

Symptom

You ask a rotund little stranger for directions. Being annoyed by his lack of reply, and the way his stupid froglike mouth is gaping at you, you punch him in the face and break your knuckles.

Possible cause

You have just assaulted a pillar box.

Symptom
Exceptionally heavy rain is falling at intermittent intervals. Other people seem unaffected by it.

Possible cause
You are walking through the fountains.

Symptom
The bus home is already waiting for you at the stop, but after standing in it for over half an hour it still hasn't moved off.

Possible cause
You are in a phone box.

Symptom
You eventually get home and fall drunkenly into bed. Your wife is not wearing curlers and greets you with a sexy smile.

Possible cause
You are in the wrong house.

I'M SORRY.
YOU'VE HAD
ENOUGH!